We Lived

in a

Little

Cabin

in the Yard

Other Books by Belinda Hurmence

FICTION

Tough Tiffany
A Girl Called Boy
Tancy
The Nightwalker
Dixie in the Big Pasture

NONFICTION

My Folks Don't Want Me to Talk about Slavery
Before Freedom, When I Just Can Remember

We Lived
in a Little Cabin
in the Yard

Edited by
Belinda Hurmence

John F. Blair, Publisher
Winston-Salem, North Carolina

Eighth Printing 2006

DESIGN BY DEBRA LONG HAMPTON
MANUFACTURED BY R. R. DONNELLEY & SONS

Photograph on front cover:
From the Penn School Collection,
courtesy of Penn Center, Inc.,
St. Helena Island, South Carolina

*The paper in this book meets the guidelines
for permanence and durability of the
Committee on Production Guidelines for
Book Longevity of the Council on Library Resources.*

Library of Congress Cataloging-in-Publication Data
We lived in a little cabin in the yard / edited by Belinda Hurmence.

  p. cm.

 ISBN 0-89587-118-1 (acid-free paper)

 1. Slaves—Virginia—Biography. 2. Slavery—Virginia.

I. Hurmence, Belinda.

E444.W35 1994

305.5'67'0922755—dc20

[B]   94–28622

For an uncommon daughter
of the commonwealth—
Harriette Hodges Andrews

Contents

Acknowledgments

Many thanks to Carolyn Sakowski, who first suggested to me the idea of editing the *Slave Narratives* of Virginia for a general readership. Thanks also to my generous friend Keppel Hagerman, for sharing with me the last will and testament of her great-great-grandfather James Derring, whose document led me to the tone I hoped to set for this book, and ultimately to the title, *We Lived in a Little Cabin in the Yard*.

I am very much indebted to Conley L. Edwards, head of Archives Public Services Section in the Virginia State

Library and Archives at Richmond, for his assistance in making available to me a number of folk histories from the WPA records, Virginia Writers Project, Life Histories, and for granting me permission to quote from those documents. The ex-slaves Baily Cunningham, Jane Pyatt, Robert Williams, and Martha Ziegler are quoted at length; brief comments are excerpted from the narratives of Archie Booker, Robert Ellett, Marriah Hines, and Louise Jones.

I also thank Michael Plunkett, director of special collections and curator of manuscripts at the University of Virginia's Alderman Library, for his assistance in making available to me the folk history of Levi Pollard, WPA Collection #1547, and for granting me permission to quote from this document.

Finally, I thank Margie Wessels, Phalbe Henriksen, and Judy Clayton at the Iredell County Library in Statesville, North Carolina, who at all times help me work out knotty problems in connection with my research, and for whose assistance with this book I am especially grateful.

Introduction

Susan Kelly, who lived her early life as a slave in Virginia, vouched for her former master. "He was good to his slaves," she says in a 1938 interview. "He never sold Mammy or us chilluns. He kept we alls together, and we lived in a little cabin in the yard."

Susan's simple words speak a history that, over the years, has been tidied up for most Americans. History books tend to focus on the politics of slavery, or its economics, and tactfully skirt the human mechanics of that unseemly institution. In the same vein, historical fiction mainly presents a romanticized or stereotypical version of slave life. The firsthand experience of a Susan Kelly, eyewitness of day-to-day life under the yoke, offers a better seminar to readers who would inform themselves about the realities of slavery.

But how to learn the firsthand experience? Susan Kelly and her fellows in slavery are long gone. By law, slaves were kept illiterate, so there is scant possibility of some lost memoir of a slave novelist/historian surfacing at this late date. Would that we might come upon such a treasure.

Luckily, we possess the equivalent in the Library of Congress. A monumental trove it is, too—some twenty-two hundred testimonies of former slaves, collected as a make-work research and writing project back in the Great Depression of the 1930s, under the auspices of the Works Progress Administration.

The method the WPA devised for this project seems incredibly primitive to present-day scholars. Even elementary students, schooled in the operation of computers and electronic recording devices, may approach the gathering of oral history with aplomb. In the 1930s, workers assigned to collect the *Slave Narratives*, as the WPA project came to be designated, were simply provided a list of questions, to which they wrote out their subjects' answers by hand. Later, they typed up their notes to fit a prescribed style.

In the state of Virginia, a few workers managed to capture the voices of some former slaves by the rudimentary recording then available to them. The idea was laudable; the recordings themselves are almost unintelligible, and so of limited value. Fortunately, typewritten text accompanied the technology of the time.

At the close of the WPA project, in which seventeen states participated, the Library of Congress organized the folk histories by state for deposit in its Rare Book and Special Collections Division. The breakdown of narratives ranges from a paltry 3 obtained in Kansas to the 677 narratives amassed by workers in Arkansas. Virginia contributed only 15.

The commonwealth's participation was far greater than the 15 would appear to indicate. Virginia's venerable Hampton Institute early assigned a zealous task force to the WPA project, and these workers continued interviewing for some months beyond termination of the federal initiative. The institute secured upwards of 300 records of former slaves. These accounts have since been published verbatim in works of immense benefit to historians and scholars.

The distinction between narratives collected specifically for the federal project and narratives gathered by Hampton as an independent undertaking is shadowy—if any distinction exists at all. Nevertheless, I decided to restrict my editing of Virginia narratives to those contained in the WPA collection, as more in keeping with my prior work— *My Folks Don't Want Me to Talk about Slavery* (1984) and *Before Freedom, When I Just Can Remember* (1989), the former consisting of selections from the North Carolina

Narratives and the latter a companion volume of South Carolina accounts.

However, not all of the fifteen Virginia histories met one or another of the standards which I wanted for *We Lived in a Little Cabin in the Yard*. My criterion of gender balance, for example. And of course, I wished to select for content as well as region, the latter meant to reveal the pervasive similarities of slave experience.

Above all, to reduce the risk of hearsay, I sought statements from those ex-slaves who had been eighty or older at the time of the WPA interviews. It seemed to me that these older ex-slaves more reliably told of vivid, personally observed events and customs, whereas the reminiscences of younger persons were often laced with the tales of acquaintances and kin but lacking in direct experience.

To prepare a representative number of the fifteen Virginia narratives for publication would have resulted in a woefully abbreviated volume, had I not hit upon the idea of extending my search for appropriate material throughout the other sixteen states in the WPA collection. Following this scheme, I have drawn nine accounts from the Alabama, Arkansas, Missouri, and Texas collections for use in *Little Cabin*. The nine constitute a unique group which I believe can rightfully be characterized as Virginia narratives. These are histories of Virginia-born slaves who had been relocated for various reasons: one sold south to another state and remaining there after Freedom, for instance; another hustled out of Virginia to prevent his escape with

Union soldiers; and so on. The testimony of these "transplanted" slaves indicates that their experience of bondage relates primarily to Virginia, and for the purposes of *Little Cabin*, I arbitrarily return their words to their home state.

In addition, I include in *Little Cabin* one manuscript account from the University of Virginia's WPA collection in the Alderman Library and four from the Virginia State Library and Archives, in Richmond.

■

The slave dwelling, situated typically in the yard and behind the "big house," had become, by the 1930s, one of the few remaining artifacts of slavery in the United States. For years following Freedom, as the *Slave Narratives* disclose, many rural ex-slaves, unaccustomed as they were to liberty and nervous about their future, continued to live much as they always had, on their former masters' plantations. Then, as gradually they gained the confidence to move out and onward, dilapidated slave quarters either became stock sheds, storage buildings, or housing for tenant farmers, or rotted away and were knocked down.

In cities, the same recycling and razing took place. Many a slave hut behind a city dwelling was turned into a downscale rental property or, more often, a "servant house" for help willing to do house or yard work in exchange for occupancy. Today, at the brink of the twenty-first century, the once-ubiquitous little cabin has virtually disappeared, except for carefully preserved or restored specimens on the great antebellum plantations of the South. A loss indeed, this poignant symbol of family unity in a culture legally deprived of its family ties.

■

Of all the afflictions visited upon black slavery in the United States—the grinding labor, the sexual abuse, the punishments, etc.—perhaps none was so cruelly imposed as the separation of families. Even a compassionate master who kept his slaves together, as Susan Kelly's did, had no compunction about splitting up slave families when it came to ensuring equity among his own children.

In his last will and testament, recorded in Isle of Wight County in 1785, James Derring left instructions for the disposition of his slaves: "I give and bequeath unto my Daughter Elizabeth Derring during her Natural life the following Negroes—Jane, Sarah, Sam, and Nelly, and after her death to her Lawfull Issue, and if she Dye without Such issue, my Will is that the said negroes be equally divided among all my children and their heirs."

Their precarious status was not lost on the slaves. "All us slaves was divided up," says Louise Jones, once a slave of Louis Merriday in Dinwiddie County. "Yes, child, some of them sold away before the old heads died. My mistess's slaves, like land and property, went to the heirs." Jones turns bitter as she laments her increased vulnerability at Freedom: "And when things was settle up, they didn't give me sweat off the black cat's eye. No, didn't give me nothing."

Withal, we may read over and over some astonishing tributes from the former slaves.

"I lived with good people, my white folks treated us good," declares Marriah Hines, former slave of James Pressman of South Hampton.

"My mistess was a nice woman. In fact, she was an angel," says Robert Ellett of Sweet Hill.

"In all the years since the war I cannot forget old Massa. He was good and kind," says Gus Brown, who as the body servant of William Brown of Richmond fought beside him at Manassas Gap.

"Sometimes I think slavery was better than freedom," says Archie Booker, former slave of Gus Crenshaw of Charles City.

Slavery better than freedom? The reader should keep in mind that Booker speaks from old age and possible infirmity, and certainly at a distant remove from slavery. At the time of his interview, harsh depression gripped the country. He may well have looked back wistfully upon healthy, carefree childhood days. And his words may echo the sentiments of other former slaves when he remembers, "If you was sick, you had a doctor. Then you got food, too. But now if you get sick and you ain't got no money, you just die. That's all!"

■

I have not corrected grammar in editing the narratives of *Little Cabin*. I have corrected misspellings and exaggerations used in the originals to convey dialect, and I have eliminated repetitious material. I have also reorganized passages to achieve a chronological sequence. At the opening of each narrative, I include as much information about the subject as the original manuscript provides and, in some cases, collateral comment, usually from the interviewer. Bracketed material within the text explains or elaborates on certain words, phrases, or expressions that might baffle the modern reader.

Belinda Hurmence

We Lived
in a
Little
Cabin
in the Yard

Charles Crawley

Age unknown;
born before the Civil War.
Interviewed February 20, 1937,
by Susie Byrd in Petersburg.

The titles "master" and "mistress" are
spelled variously throughout the *Slave
Narratives*, no doubt owing to individual
pronunciation. Crawley says "marster,"
"Marse," "mistess," and "mis."

God knows how old I am. All I know is, I was born before the war. Yes, I was a slave and belonged to a family of Allens in Lunenburg County. They owned about fifty head of colored people. Marster Allen owned my mother and sister, too.

We used to call Marster Allen, Colonel Allen. His name was Robert. He was a home general, and a lawyer, too. When he went to court, any slave he said to free was freed and turned a-loose. The white folks as well as slaves obeyed Marster Allen.

We had plenty of food, such as it was—cornbread, buttermilk, sweet potatoes, in weekdays. On Sunday we had biscuits, and sometimes a little extra food, which old Mistess would send out to Mother for us.

All the work I did was to play and drive cows, being

only a boy—worked around as chillun, doing this and that—little things the white folks would call me to do.

For clothing, we were allowed two suits a year—one for spring and one for winter was all you had. The underclothes were made at home. Underclothes made out of sacks and bags. You also got two pairs of shoes and homemade hats and caps. Our summer hats were made out of plaited straw. The white folks, or your slave owners, would teach them who could catch on easy, and they would teach the other slaves, and that's how they kept all slaves clothed.

You said something about how we served God. Marster's slaves met and worshiped from house to house, and honey, we talked to God all us wanted. You would get a remit [master's handwritten pass] to go to these places. You would have to show your remit. If the pattyrollers [patrollers; a local policing body, or patrol] caught you, they would whip you. That's the way they done in them days.

Pattyrollers is a gang of white men getting together going through the country catching slaves, and whipping and beating them up if they had no remit.

If slaves rebelled, I done seed them whip them with a strop called "cat-nine-tails." Honey, this strop was about broad as your hand, from thumb to little finger, and it was cut in strips up. You done seen these whips that they whip horses with? Well, they was used, too.

When slaves ran away, they were brought back to their marster and mistess. Well, if these slaves was caught, they were sold by their new marsters to go down south. There was a auction block I saw right here in Petersburg, on the corner of Sycamore Street and Bank Street. Slaves were auctioned off to the highest bidder. Lord! Lord! I done seen them younguns fought and kick like crazy folks. Child, it was pitiful to see them.

They tell me them marsters down south was so mean to slaves they would let them work them cotton fields till they fall dead with hoes in their hands, and would beat them. . . . I don't like to talk about back there. It brung a sad feeling up me. I'm glad to say we had good owners. Marster Allen wouldn't allow no one to whip and beat his slaves, and he would handle anybody if they did.

Did you know poor whites like slaves had to get a pass? I mean, remit, like us slaves, to sell anything and to go places, or do anything. Just as we colored people, they had to go to some big white man like Colonel Allen, they did. If Marster wanted to, he would give them a re-mit, or pass; and if he didn't feel like it, he wouldn't do it. Old Marster was more hard on them poor white folks than he was on us niggers.

I don't know but two sets of white folks slaves up my way; one was name Chatman, and the other one Hollovies. These two families worked on Allen's farm as we did. Off from us on a plot called Morgan's Lot there, they lived as slaves just like us colored folks.

Yes, the poor white man had some dark and tough days, like us poor niggers, I mean—were lashed and treated, some of them, just as pitiful and unmerciful. Lord, Lord, baby! I hope you young folks will never know what slavery is, and will never suffer as your foreparents. I'm living to tell the tale to you, honey. Yes, Jesus, you've spared me. My marster and mistess was good to me as well as all us slaves.

Oh, yes, honey, I can remember when the Yankees came into this town; they broke in stores and told all the niggers to go in and get anything they wanted.

We emigrant here, came to this town of Petersburg after Lee's surrender—I mean, you know, the ending of the Civil War. Mis and Marse Allen didn't want us to leave that part of the country to come to this here place down the road, but we comed ourselves to make a home for ourselves.

My mother, sister, and I came on down the road in a boxcar which stopped outside the outskirts; it didn't go through the city. Yes, I know when the first railroads were built, the Norfolk and Western and the Atlantic Coast Line; they were run through Petersburg, and in them days it was called the Southern.

Well, now, we worked here and there, with this here man and that man, with different people till we bought us a home and paid for it. The ground was bought from a lady, colored, name Sis Jackey, and she was sometimes called in them days the Mother of Harrison Street Baptist Church. I reckon this church is the oldest one in Petersburg.

Mother died right here in this here house, twelve years

ago this coming March eleventh. I am yet living in this same house that she and us all labored and worked for by the sweat of our brow, and with these hands. Child, them days was some days.

For as I think, if slavery had lasted it would have been pretty tough. As it was some fared good, while others fared common—you know, slaves who were beat and treated bad. God is punishing some of them old suckers and their chillun right now for the way they used to treat us poor colored folks.

I think by Negro getting educated he has profited, and this here younger generation is going to take nothing off these here poor white folks when they don't treat them right, because now this country is a free country; no slavery now.

Susan Kelly

Age 100 when interviewed
in 1938 by Lucille B. Wayne
in the upper part of Guinea, known
to local residents as "The Hook."

My mammy, Anna Burrell, was a slave, her massa was Colonel Hayes, of Woodwell; he was good to his slaves. He never sold Mammy or us chilluns; he kept we alls together, and we lived in a little cabin in the yard. Mammy used to bake ashcakes. They was made with meal, with a little salt, and mixed with water. Then Mammy would rake up the ashes in the fireplace; then she would make up the meal in round cakes and put them on the hot bricks to bake. When they had cooked around the edges, she would put ashes on the top of them, and when they was nice and brown, she took them out and washed them off with water.

My job was minding Massa's and Missus's chilluns all day long, and putting them to bed at night. They had to have a story told to them before they would go to sleep, and the baby had to be rocked before she would go to sleep, and I had to sing for her:

Rock-a-bye, baby, close them eyes,
Before old sand man comes;
Rock-a-bye, baby, don't let old sand man
Catch you peeping.

Mammy said it was very bad luck to meet a woman early in the morning walking; and never carry back salt that you have borrowed, for it will bring bad luck to you and to the one you brung it to.

For a hawk to fly over the house is sure a sign of death, for the hawk will call corpses when he flies over.

Baily Cunningham

Age about 99 when interviewed
March 14, 1938, by I. M. Warren of Roanoke.

My mother and my grandmother were slaves. My grandfather Cunningham was a white man. He came from the old country, Germany, and brought my grandmother, a colored woman, with him.

My mother belonged to Bemis English, who had a large plantation about eleven miles from Rocky Mount, Virginia, in Franklin County. Our master was a rich man. He had a store and a sawmill on the creek. When I was a boy he had about seventy-five slaves, including the children. My mother kept house for our missus and looked after the quarters and reported anything going wrong to the missus.

The cabins were built in two rows not very far from the missus's big house. They were log cabins; some had one room and some had two rooms, and board floors. The cabins were covered with boards, nailed on, and had stick-and-mud chimneys.

We had homemade tables and chairs with wooden bottoms. We had homemade beds, corded, with mattresses made of linen filled with straw, and pillows the same, and a woolen or cotton blanket.

We never went to school or to church. We didn't know but one holiday, that was Christmas day, and it was not much different from any other day. The field hands did not have to work on Christmas day. We didn't have any Christmas presents.

A sick slave was reported to the missus. She had three kinds of medicine that would cure everything. One was vinegar nail, one rosin pills, and the other was tar. When we had aches or pains in the stomach or the back she would make us drink vinegar nail, which was made by getting about a pound of square-cut iron nails and put them in a jug with a lot of vinegar; then at night we had to take two rosin pills. These pills were made of raw pine rosin. When we had the toothache or the earache, she would fill the tooth or ear full of tar. We never had a doctor.

Rations were given to the field hands every Monday morning. They would go to the smokehouse and the missus would give us some meal and meat in our sack. On Saturday morning we would go to the smokehouse and get a piece of meat with a bone and some flour so we could have a hoecake for dinner on Sunday.

We had a large iron baker with a lid to bake bread and potatoes and a large iron kettle to boil things in. We were allowed to go to the garden or field and get cabbage, potatoes, and corn or any other vegetables and cook in our shanties. Sometimes we had plenty of milk and coffee.

We ate twice a day, about sunup and at sundown. All the work hands ate in the cabins, and all the children took their simlin [gourd] soup bowl to the big kitchen and got it full of cabbage soup, then we were allowed to go to the table where the white folks ate and get the crumbs from the table. We sat on the ground around the quarters to eat with wooden spoons.

All the boys and girls wore shirt tails until we were twenty. It was a long garment that came down to the knees. The boys and girls never wore but one garment even in the winter time. It was made large and out of cotton, flax, or wool on the old loom which was kept going all the year.

I never had a hat or shoes until I was twenty. The field hands had wooden-sole shoes. The wooden bottom was made of maple, the size of the foot, one-half inch thick or thicker, and the leather nailed to the wood.

After they were twenty they had to work on the plantation or be sold out [hired out, a fairly common practice] by our master. I was sold to a hotel man in Lynchburg soon after I was twenty for one year for $125. I remember well, as I had never had on britches or a suit of clothes until I went to Lynchburg. I did not work in the field until I came home from Lynchburg.

All the field hands our master did not need on the plantation were sold [hired out] to the tobacco factories at Lynchburg. The stray slaves wandering about were taken up by the traders and held until he had about a hundred, then they were sold and taken to the southern cotton fields. They were chained together, a chain fastened to the arm of each one, and they went afoot to North Carolina, South Carolina, or Georgia, driven by their new master.

We played around the quarters, and played Hide the Switch most of the time. They had big dances at night, sometimes. Somebody would play the fiddle and some the banjo and sometimes had a drum. We did the buck dance. A boy and girl would hold hands and jump up and down and swing around, keeping time with the music.

We would dance awhile, then go to the other room and drink coffee, corn whiskey, or apple brandy. Sometimes some of us would get drunk. We would dance and play all night but had to be ready to work next day.

We had to get a pass from our master or missus to go to the dance, as we were afraid the pattyrollers would get us. The master would have eight or ten men on horses watching, and anyone caught without a pass was taken up and punished, sometimes whipped.

The day the stars fell, I was eight years old, but I remember it as well as if it was yesterday. They began to fall about sundown and fell all night. They fell like rain. They looked like little balls about as big as marbles with a long streak of fire to them. They fell everywhere, but you couldn't hear them. They did not hit the ground, or the house. We were all scared and did not go out of the house but could see them everywhere. A few days later it began to snow and snowed three days and nights. The snow piled up over some of the houses; some people froze and some starved.

■

[Numerous other references in the *Slave Narratives* confirm Cunningham's recollection of what must have been a spectacular meteor shower. The length and brilliance of the occurrence took on supernatural significance for many who witnessed it.]

Joseph Holmes

Age 81 when interviewed
near Prichard, Alabama,
in June 1937.

I was born in Henry County, Virginny, near Danville. My ma's name was Liza Rowlets, and my daddy's name was Joseph Holmes. My daddy had the same name as the people what owned him.

My ma had eight chillun, and we was raised in pairs. I had a sister who come along with me, and if I jumped in the river to swim she did it, too; if I clum a tree or went through a briar patch she done it right behind me. Ma wanted to know why her clothes was so tore up, and we'd make it right with Ma by having a rabbit or coon with us, and sometimes a mud turtle.

Lord, my white folks was rich; they had as many as five or six hundred niggers, men, women, and chillun. The plantation was big, but I don't remember how many acres. I does remember the cabins was all built in rows, and streets was laid out between the cabins. Us had home-made beds with two sides nailed to the wall, and the mattresses was made out of wheat straw. The chimneys was built out of dirt and sticks.

You know, up in Virginny it got terrible cold, and the snow would pile up, so when the cabins was built the men throwed dirt up under the house to keep the snow and cold out. You might think that dirt would wash out from under the house, but it didn't. It just made them so warm and comfortable, we didn't suffer.

Folks was a heap kinder-hearted than they is now; they kept big dogs to hunt up people lost in the snow. They all seemed more happy, because they was all busy. At night, instead of wasting they time, they would go to the big house and spin and weave and make clothes.

I can hear that old loom humming now, and see great cards of cloth coming out; and them was *clothes* then, that was made from it. It took fire to get them off of you, they was so strong. I doesn't remember what they used for dye, but I know they used copperas as sizing to hold the colors. Some of the cloth was dyed red, blue, and black.

They not only made our clothes, but also made our hats. Of course they wasn't very hatty, but was more cappy. They made them with tabs over the ears, and to tie under the chin, and was they warm—I'll say!

Old Miss taught the niggers how to read and write, and some of them got to be too efficient with the writing— they learn how to write too many passes so the pattyrollers wouldn't get them. That was the onliest time I ever knowed old Miss to have the slaves punished. Oh, once in a while old Miss might slap the cook's face and tell her to bear down round there, and if she wanted the serving boys to hurry she would say, "Cutch it," meaning for them to cut some steps and get about in a hurry.

Old Miss never allowed no mistreating the slaves. They was raising slaves for the market, and it wouldn't be good business to mistreat them. I really thought Old Miss was a angel. I remember every Sunday morning that she made the older slaves bring all the little niggers up to her big white two-story house, so she could read the Bible to us; and then she give us plenty them good biscuits and taters that she had the cook, Susanne, cook for us. She'd say, "Get around there, Susanne, and help them little niggers' plates."

Lord, honey, Virginny is the best place on earth for good eating and good white folks. You wouldn't believe the fruit us did have! Such as apples, cherries, quinces, peaches, and pears. It makes my mouth water to think about them Cheese apples that was yellow like gold, and those Abraham apples, the like of which ain't now to be had. And those cherry trees as big as these oaks, with long limbs, and Big Sugar and Sweetheart and Black Heart cherries. Then there was another kind of cherry called the Gorilla, that was round and growed as big as the yellow plums down this way.

Now, let me tell you something about Virginny. It had its own law about drink. They made the best peach and cherry brandy, and most any kind you ever heard of, 'cepting they didn't allow you to make drink out of any-thing you could make into bread, such as corn and rye.

Us had our brandy same as you would coffee, because it was cold, and some mornings us would get up and the snow would be halfway up the door, and the men would have to ditch it out, so us could get out of the house. On them real cold mornings my daddy would get the brandy out and my ma would put a little water and sugar with it and give to us chillun. And then she'd take some in her mouth and put it in the baby's mouth, and it would open its eyes and stamp its foot real peart like.

Now, you asked about hog-killing time—that was the time of times! For weeks the men would haul wood and big rocks and pile it all together as high as that house, then have several piles like these around a big hole in the ground what had been filled with water. Then just a little after midnight the boss would blow the old horn, and all the men would get up and get in them hog pens. Then they would set that pile of wood on fire, and then start knocking them hogs in the head. Us never shot a hog like they does now. Us always used an ax to kill them with.

After knocking the hog in the head they would tie a rope on its leg, and after the water got to the right heat, from those red-hot rocks what had been pushed into the water, they would throw the hog in and drag it around awhile, and take him out and have him clean in about three pair of minutes. After he was clean they hung him up, and then later cut him up and hung him in the smokehouse, and smoke him with great oak logs. Huh, they don't cure meat now; they just use some kind of liquid to brush over it. We used to have sure-enough meat.

Then come corn-shucking time. My goodness, I just would love to be there now. The corn would be piled up high and one man would get on that pile. It usually was one who was a kind of nigger foreman, that could sing and get the work out of the other niggers. This foreman would sing a verse something like this:

Polk and Clay went to war,
And Polk come back with a broken jaw.

Then all the niggers would sing back to him, and holler, a kind of shouting sound. Generally this foreman made up his songs by picking them up from what he had heard white folks tell of wars. I wish I could remember those old songs, but all that holler done left me. The onliest singing I hears now is the good old sisters singing and saying "Amen."

But miss, you know what was the motor power of that corn shucking? It was the old jug that was brung around every hour. That's the onliest time any of the slaves really got drunk. Us never thought nothing of drinking. I kinda believe like that old infidel, Ingersoll, who said that anything that was the custom, was the religion. [Robert Ingersoll was a flamboyant orator known as "the great agnostic."]

I seed General Grant's army when it went through Virginny. Just as sure as you is standing there, lady, I seed him, and I seed them men all dressed in them blue suits a-marching side by side, going down the road past our place. It took them three days to get past our house.

And do I remember when them Yankees come to old Miss's house and took a ladder and climb up to the roof and tear the boards out of the ceiling, to get them big hams and shoulders they had hid up there? I sure do. The women folks makes the slaves hide the meat; and when them Yankees find that stuff, they just give it all to the niggers. And I remember, too, how old Miss calls us all to her after they left and told us that us was free, but she told us that us have to give back the meat and preserves, because she didn't have a bit to eat. 'Course we was glad to do it, cause old Miss sure was good to her slaves.

If anybody tells you that the white folks was mean to their niggers, they never come from Virginny. Us was too near the free states, and I done already told you that they raised niggers to sell and they kept them in good conditions. In those days white folks was white folks and black folks was black folks. Just like Booker T. Washington was a river between the niggers of this generation and learning. He had all that was fine and good, and he give the best to his people, if they would take it. That was the way with the white folks, then; they didn't do no whipping.

Talking about niggers being freed, old Miss told us us

was free, but it was ten or twelve years after the surrender before I knowed what she was talking about. I was a big boy going to school before I had any understanding as to what she meant.

I's the oldest rat in the pond, and because I ain't hung in the smokehouse, folks think I's not as old as I says I is, but child, I's been here. I remember how black Sam used to preach to us, when we was at old Miss's place, and when I growed up I remember how I used to think nobody was a Christian excepting us Baptists, but I know better now. And the longer I live, the more I realize that the churches go away because they leave off the ordinance of God, though us has got the Bible and more Christian literature than ever before.

In days gone by I went to plenty of dances and candy pullings, but I don't do that any more. I's a preacher, and when I first left Virginny I come to Georgia, and I kicked up a-plenty of dust in Georgia. Then I come on to Alabammy. I's been a square citizen, and there hasn't been but one time in my life I's had to call on anybody, and that was when I had to call on Uncle Sam, when old man Depression got me. But thank God I's still able to be about and have all my faculties, excepting my eyesight is a little poorly. I still has all my teeth, excepting one, and my ma always took pride in my hair—you see how fine and silky it is, and it ain't snow-white yet.

There is one thing to be thankful for. That is because I's so near home.

Robert Williams

Age 94 when interviewed
May 8, 1937, by William T. Lee
at 63 Taylor Street in Lynchburg.

I was owned by Clinton Clay of Forest, Virginia. He gave the land to the railroad when they was building through here. That's the reason they call it Clay's Crossing on the Norfolk and Western, between Lynchburg and Forest.

I seen them sell slaves on the block down on Ninth Street in Lynchburg. They used to give us pass to come to town on Saturday sometime, and that is how I got to see the sale.

The block was a big rock that slaves would stand on so they would be up over the crowd. The seller would cry bids just like they sell tobacco: "$150, who will make it $160?" and so on. Some of the bids would start as high as $400, according to the condition of the person.

The women would have just a piece around her waist, her breast and thighs would be bare. The seller would have her turn around and plump her to show how fat she was and her general condition. They would also take her by her breasts and pull them to show how good she was built for raising chillun. They would have them examined to show they was in good health. The young women would bring good money, such as $1,000 or more, because they could have plenty chillun, and that where they profit would come in.

They sold my cousin and sent her down in the cotton fields of the deep South, because Master got short of money. After the war was over we heard from her, and she was raising cotton for herself and making a living.

I done seen groups of slaves—women, men, and chillun—walking down the road, some of the women with babies in they arms and some on ox-carts with babies, all on they way to the cotton country. Some them would hardly have on any clothes. We lived near the road and these groups of slaves would come very often when cotton season was in. The white folks would come up from the cotton country and buy slaves and carry them back in droves.

This was before the war. I was a little boy working around the house, and sometimes these slaves would stop, because they would get sick. Some of them had on shoes and some didn't. They was just like cattle in a herd.

One day it was right cold and Master was going to whip me for something. I turned and seen him getting some switches, then I broke and ran, and ran, because I could travel. When I got to a fence I just laid one hand on the fence, and over I went.

Master hollered, "Catch him!" but I was gone.

Well, I got away and slept in the woods behind logs at nights. During the day I would hide, and at nights before I went to sleep I would go around slave quarters and get food. I got me all I wanted to eat and plenty of rest. I stayed out in the woods about a year. I wandered all around at nights. I had made up in my mind that I wasn't going take that beating that day, because the cold weather was more'n I could stand; and then to take my shirt off and get a beating was more than I was going to take.

When I was out in the woods Master put out a reward of $50 for me, but I stayed clear of everybody. I wandered over to Dr. Ned Reed's quarters. He was a slave and a hoo-doo doctor and could help me out. He told me that he could fix things up for me if I would give him a quarter, but I told him that I had been in the woods for a year and didn't have any money.

He said, "Well, I will help you, because when you do get something you can pay me." He gave me some powders and told me to sprinkle them under the door mat, and if I could to put some in Master's hat, and he couldn't bother me.

I slipped home and went round the big house one night and put some of the powders under the door mat. The next day I went on up to the house and saw the master's hat and sprinkled some in his hat.

After while Master saw me, and he said, "God damn! Where in the hell has you been and why didn't you come home?"

I told him I thought he was going to beat me. I had my eyes on a stick and he didn't know it. While I was talking to him I made up my mind to hit him if he started to whipping me.

Master told me to go down to the slave quarters and wait for him. After the slaves had all gone out he came and told me to saddle his horse, because he had to go to town. He was a lawyer and he had to come to town. When he came in the stable I thought he was going to try to beat me, but he only told me to get up to the house and do whatever they wanted me to do.

When I went up there the mistress asked me what I wanted, and I told her I came to do whatever she wanted me to do. She said she didn't want me to do nothing. When Master came he told me to go to the field. From that day on he never did bother me. I was sent to work on the railroad later on, and I was a cart driver. My master had four of his slaves hired to the railroad at $200 apiece a year.

We could have dances on Saturday nights. A banjo player would be there and he would sing. One song they used to sing was

> Run nigger run, run nigger run,
> Don't let the pattyrollers catch you.
> Run nigger run.

The niggers would be patting they feet and dancing for life. Master and them would be setting on the front porch listening to the music, because you could hear it for a half-mile. We would be in one of the big barns. We had a time of our life.

Poor whites would come over to see the dance. The master wouldn't allow the poor whites on his place, and they would have to steal in to see the dance. Whenever they would come round to the big house they had to come to the back door, and the white folks would ask them, "What in the hell do you want?" Poor whites was just like stray goats.

Just before the war started, Master had planned to sell about four of us. I remember hearing them talking about a war, and soon after that they was getting ready. This war broke out and we had to be used at home, and later we was sent to the breastworks.

I was pressed for service to make breastworks over in Amherst. We didn't have no guns. All the slaves was brought back to town each night and we was locked up in a jail that they had on Ninth Street near Commerce Street. We was put in the jail just like you would drive cattle in a barn.

I had two buttons shot off my coat. That scared me awful. General Munford led a group of soldiers in this section, and he led them right into the danger, and when the first shot was fired at them he ran. Master had two brothers in the war, and one of them got shot through the stomach, and with his guts coming out he hollered, "Fight on, boys, I am done!" I slipped over with the Yankees and stayed about three months till after the war was over.

Elizabeth Sparks

Interviewed at the courthouse
in Mathews on January 13, 1937,
by Claude J. Anderson.

My mistress's name was Miss Jennie Brown. She died about four years ago. Bless her. She was a good woman. 'Course I mean she'd slap and beat you once in a while, but she weren't no woman for fighting, fussing, and beating you all day, like some I know. 'Course no white folks perfect.

Before Miss Jennie was married, she lived at her old home right up the river here. You can see the place from outside here.

Her mother was a mean old thing. She'd beat you with a broom or a leather strap, or anything she'd get her hands on.

She used to make my aunt Caroline knit all day, and when she get so tired after dark that she'd get sleepy, she'd make her stand up and knit. She work her so hard that she'd go to sleep standing up, and every time her head nod and her knees sag, the lady'd come down across her head with a switch.

That was Miss Jennie's mother. She'd give the cook just so much meal to make bread from, and if she burnt it she'd be scared to death, because they'd whip her. I remember plenty of times the cook ask, say, "Massa, please excuse this bread; it's a little too brown." Yessir! Beat the devil out her if she burn that bread.

On the plantation my mother was a house woman. She had to wash white folks' clothes all day and hers after dark. Sometimes she'd be washing clothes way up around midnight. No sir, couldn't wash any nigger's clothes in daytime.

Shep Miller was my master. Bought my mother, a little girl, when he was married. She was a real Christian and he respected her a little. Didn't beat her so much. 'Course he beat her once in a while. Beat women! Why, sure he beat women. Beat women just like men. Beat women naked and wash them down in brine.

He was that way with them black folks. Shep Miller was terrible. Why, I remember time after he was dead when I'd peep in the closet and see his old clothes hanging there, and just fly. Yessir, I'd run from them clothes; and I was just a little girl then. No, he ain't in heaven—went past heaven.

Old Master done so much wrongness, I couldn't tell you all of it. Slave girl Betty Lilly always had good clothes and all the privileges. She was a favorite of his.

Might as well quit looking at me. I ain't going to tell you any more. Can't tell you all I know—old Shep might come back and get me. Why, if I was to tell you the really bad things, some of them dead white folks would come right up out of their graves. But can't tell all! God's got all!

■

Slaves went to bed when they didn't have anything to do. Most time they went to bed when they could. They worked six days from sun to sun. Usual work day began when the horn blow and stop when the horn blow. They get off just long enough to eat at noon. If they forcing wheat or other crops, they start to work long before day. Sometimes the men had to shuck corn till eleven and twelve o'clock at night.

Didn't have much to eat. Well, they give the colored people an allowance every week. A woman with children would get about a half-bushel of meal a week; a childless woman would get about a peck and a half of meal a week. They get some suet and slice of bread for breakfast. For dinner they'd eat ashcake baked on blade of a hoe.

The men on the road got one cotton shirt and jacket. If you was working they'd give you shoes. Children went barefooted the year around.

Schools? Son, there weren't no schools for niggers. Niggers used to go way off in quarters and slip and have meetings. They called it "stealing the meeting." If you went out at night the pattyrollers would catch you, if you was out after time without a pass. If they catch them they beat them near to death. Most of the slaves was afeared to go out.

Plenty of slaves ran away. Sometimes they beat them so bad they just couldn't stand it, and they run away to the woods. If you get in the woods they couldn't get you. You could hide and people slip you something to eat.

They had colored foremen, but they always have a white overseer. After a while, he tell one of colored foremen, tell you come on back, he ain't going beat you any more. Foreman get you to come back and then he beat you to death again. That's the way the white folks was. But you know, there's good and bad people everywhere. Some had hearts; some had gizzards instead of hearts.

I lived at Seaford then and was around fifteen or sixteen when my mistress married. I remember just as well when they gave me to Jennie. We was all in a room helping her dress, and she turns around and says to us, "Which of you niggers you think I'm going to get when I get married?"

We all say, "I don't know."

And she looks right at me and point her finger at me like this and said, "You!"

I was so glad. She was just a young thing. She didn't beat. 'Course she take a whack at me sometime, but that weren't nothing.

I went with Miss Jennie and worked at house. I didn't have to cook. I slept in my mistress's room, but I ain't slept in any bed. No sir! I slept on a carpet, an old rug, before the fireplace.

I had to get permission to go to church; everybody did. We could sit in the gallery at the white folks' service in the morning, and in the evening the folks held baptize service in the gallery with white present.

I was about nineteen when I married. My husband lived on another plantation. I got permission to get married. You always had to get permission. White folks would give you away. You jump across a broomstick together, and you was married.

I was married in 1861. My oldest boy was born in 1862, and the falling of Richmond came in 1865.

Shep went to war, but not for long. We didn't see none of it, but the slaves knew what the war was about. The slaves wanted freedom, but they's scared to tell the white folks so. They sent some of the slaves to South Carolina when the Yankees came near, to keep the Yankees from getting them. Sent Cousin James to South Carolina.

After the war they tried to fool the slaves about freedom, and wanted to keep them on a-working—white folks' heads was just going to keep on having slaves. But the Yankees told them they was free.

I never will forget when the Yankees came through. They was taking all the livestock and all the men slaves back to Norfolk with them, to break up the system. What tickled me was my husband, John Sparks. He didn't want to leave me and go, because he didn't know where they was taking them nor what they was going to do, so he played lame to keep from going. He was just a-limping around. It was all I could do to keep from laughing.

I can hear Miss Jennie now, yelling at them Yankees: "No! Who are you to judge? I'll be the judge. If John Sparks wants to stay here he'll stay."

They was going to take him anyhow, and he went inside to pack, and the baby started crying. So one of them said that as long as he had a wife and a baby that young, they guessed he could stay.

Anyway, the Yankees was giving everything to the slaves. I can hear them telling old Mistress now, "Yes! Give her clothes. Let her take anything she wants."

They even took some of Miss Jennie's things and offered them to me. I didn't take them, though, because she'd been pretty nice to me. They took all the horses, cows, and pigs and chickens and anything they could use and left.

When my mother's master died he called my mother and brother Major and got religion and talked so pretty. He say he so sorry that he hadn't found the Lord before and had nothing against his colored people. He was sorry and scared, but confessed.

Now, you take that and go. Put that in the book. You can make out with that. It ain't no sense for you to know about all those mean white folks. They meant good, I reckon. They all dead now. Leastways, most of them got salvation on their death beds.

The end of time is at hand, anyway. The Bible say when it gets so you can't tell one season from the other, the world's coming to end. Here it is, so warm in winter that it feels like summer.

Elige Davison

Age unknown.
Living with one of his grandsons
in Madisonville, Texas.

My birth was in Richmond. That's over in old Virginny, and George Davison owned me and my pappy and mammy. I remember one sister, named Felina Tucker.

Massa and Missus were very good white folks and was good to the black folks. They had a great big rock house with pretty trees all around it, but the plantation was small, not more'n a hundred acres. Massa growed tobacco on 'bout thirty of them acres, and he had a big bunch of hogs. He waked us up about four in the morning to milk the cows and feed them and us. Us work all day till just before dark.

Our quarters was good, builded out of pine logs, with a bed in the corner, no floors and windows. Us wore old loyal clothes [Lowell cloth, a cotton fabric named for a textile manufacturer], and our shirt was open all down the front. In winter Massa gave us woolen clothes to wear. We didn't know what shoes was, though.

Massa learn us to read and us read the Bible. He learn us to write, too. They had a big church on the plantation and us go to church and learn to tell the truth.

Us couldn't go to nowhere without a pass. The pattyrollers would get us and they do plenty for nigger slave. I's went to my quarters and be so tired I just fall in the door, on the ground, and a pattyroller come by and hit me several licks with a cat-o'-nine-tails, to see if I's tired enough to not run away. Sometimes them pattyrollers hit us just to hear us holler.

Massa, he look after us slaves when us sick, because us worth too much money to let die just like you do a mule. He get doctor or nigger mammy. She make tea out of weeds, better'n quinine. She put string round the neck for chills and fever, with camphor on it. That sure keep off diseases.

Sometimes us got whippings. We didn't mind so much. Boss, you know how stubborn a mule am, he have to be whipped. That the way slaves is. I seed some few run away to the North, and Massa sometime catch them and put them in jail.

I been marry once before freedom, with home wedding. Massa, he bring some more women to see me. He wouldn't let me have just one woman. I have about fifteen and I don't know how many chillun. Some over a hundred, I's sure.

When you gather a bunch of cattle to sell they calves, how the calves and cows will bawl, that the way the slaves was then. They didn't know nothing about they kinfolks.

Most chillun didn't know who they pappy was and some they mammy, 'cause they taken away from the mammy when she wean them, and sell or trade the chillun to someone else, so they wouldn't get attached to they mammy or pappy.

When a slave die he just another dead nigger. Massa, he builded a wooden box and put the nigger in and carry him to the hole in the ground. Us march round the grave three times and that all.

I remember plenty about the war, because the Yankees, they march on to Richmond. They kill everything what in the way. I heared them big guns and I's scared. Everybody scared. I didn't see no fighting, because I gets out the way and keeps out till it all over.

But when they marches right on the town, I's tending hosses for Massa. He have two hosses kilt right under him. Then the Yankees, they capture that town. Massa, he send me to get the buggy and horse and carry Missus to the mountain, but them Yankees, they capture me and say they going hang that nigger. But glory be, Massa, he saves me before they hangs me. He send he wife and my wife to another place then, because they burn Massa's house and tear down all he fences.

When the war over Massa call me and tells me I's free as he was, because them Yankees win the war. Most niggers just got turn loose with a cuss, and not enough clothes to cover they bodies. I didn't get no land or mule or cow. They weren't no plantations divided what I knowed about.

He give me five dollars and say he'll give me that much a month if I stayed with him, but I starts to Texas. I heared I wouldn't have to work in Texas, because everything growed on trees and the Texans wore animal hides for clothes.

It about a year before I gets to Texas. I walks nearly all the way. Sometimes I get a little ride with farmer. Sometimes I work for folks along the way and get fifty cents and start again.

I got to Texas and try to work for white folks and try to farm. I couldn't make anything at any work. I made five dollars a month for I don't know how many year after the war. If the woods wasn't full of wild game us niggers all starve to death them days.

I been marry three time. First wife Eve Shelton. She run off with another man. Then I marries Fay Elly. Us separate in a year. Then I marry Parlee Breyle. No, I done forgot. Before that I marries Sue Wilford, and us have seven gals and six boys. They all in New York but one. He stays here. Then I marries Parlee and us have two gals. Parlee die three year ago.

The government give me a pension and I gets little odd jobs round, to get by. But times been hard and I ain't had much to eat the last few years. Not near so good as what old Massa done give me. But I gets by somehow.

I done the best I could, considering I's turned out with nothing when I's growed, and didn't know much, neither. The young folks, they knows more, because they got the chance for schooling.

Henry Johnson

Age estimated at 90-plus
when interviewed at his dwelling
at 1526 Hanley Road, Lincoln Terrace,
in St. Louis, Missouri, by Grace E. White.

Johnson showed the writer scars
on his head and shoulders,
which he said resulted from
the beatings he describes in his account.

My name is Henry Johnson. I was born in Patrick County, Virginia, and was raised all over the state. I was only sold twice. My father's name was Bill Alexander and my mother's name was Fannie, but I didn't know nothing about my parents till I was past eighteen years old, or about that. I never knowed my real age. My owner's name was Billy Johnson in Patrick County, so I always carried his name.

My boss had eleven children. He had 125 slaves on one of the plantations, 200 on another. On all his plantations he owned better'n 1,500 slaves. He was one of the richest landowners in the state of Virginia. I stayed with that family until way after the war was fought.

When I was a little bit a fellow I used to pack water to twenty-five and thirty men in one field, then go back to the house and bring enough water for breakfast the next morning. When I got a little bigger I had to take a little hoe and dig weeds out of the crop. If our white boss see a little grass we overlooked he would handcuff our feet to a whipping post, then chain the slave around the stomach to the post and strap the chin over the top of the post and place your hands in front of you.

In the start the slave has been stripped naked and lashed, often to death. They would be left strapped after from twenty-five to fifty lashes every two or three hours to stand there all night. The next day the overseer would be back with a heavy paddle full of holes, that had been dipped in boiling water, and beat until the whole body was full of blisters. Then he'd take a cat-and-nine-tails dipped in hot salt water to draw out the bruised blood and would open every one of them blisters with that. If the slave did not die from that torture he would be unfastened from the whipping post and made go to the field just as he was. Often times he would die shortly after. They did the women the same.

I never knowed what a shirt was until I was past twenty. I only went to school three days in my whole life, but a colored friend taught me how to spell out of a blue-back spelling book. His name was Charlie Snowball. I was learning fine until I got burned. Then my eyesight was poor for a long time, but I see now very good. I only need glasses for to read what little I can read. I can't write at all.

When my young master went three miles to school he

rode on a horse; I had to walk alongside the horse to carry his books, then go home and fetch him a hot dinner for noon and go back after him at night to carry them books.

They would take a great string of slaves in the road on Sunday and make us walk to church. Buggies with the white folks in would be in front of us, in the midst of us, and all betwixt and behind us. When we got that four or five miles we had to sit on a log in the broiling sun while a white man preached to us. All they ever would say would be, "Niggers, obey your masters and mistess and don't steal from them."

And lo and behold, honey, the masters would make us slaves steal from each of the slave owners. Our master would make us surround a herd of his neighbor's cattle, round them up at night, and make us slaves stay up all night long and kill and skin every one of them critters, salt the skins down in layers in the master's cellar, and put the cattle piled ceiling-high in the smokehouse, so nobody could identify skinned cattle.

Then when the sheriff would come around looking for all them stolen critters, our boss would say, "Sheriff, just go right on down to them niggers' cabins and search them good; I know my niggers don't steal."

'Course the sheriff come to our cabins and search; sure we didn't have nothing didn't belong to us—but the boss had plenty. After the sheriff's search we had to salt and smoke all that stolen meat and hang it in Master's smokehouse for him. Then they tell us, "Don't steal"!

They raised turkeys in the five hundred lots and never did give us one. So we wanted one so bad once, I put corn underneath the cabin and a turkey, a great big one, would come under our cabin to eat that corn. One day when I got a chance I caught that old gobbler by the neck and him and me went round and round under that old cabin house.

He was the biggest, strongest bird I ever see. I was only a boy but finally I beat. I twisted his neck till he died. Then I took out up to the big house, fast as anything, to tell my old mistess one of our finest turkeys dead. She said, "Stop crying, Henry, and throw him under the hill."

I was satisfied. I run back, picked that old bird, taken all his feathers to the river, and throwed them in. That night we cooked him, and didn't we eat something good! I had to tell her about that missing bird, because when they check up it all had to tally; so that fixed that.

My old master told me when the war was being fought and the Yankees was on the way, coming through Franklin County, Virginia, "My little nigger, do you know how old you is?" I said, "No sir, boss." He said, "You are seventeen years old." He often told me I was born just one hour before his youngest son.

I never even saw my mother and father until I was in my twenties. This was after the war was over. A white man taken me to Danville, Virginia, to drive his carriage for him. After I was there a spell a colored man kept watching me so much I got plumb scared. Then one day, lo and behold, he jumped at me and he grabbed me and asked me where I was staying. I did not know whether to tell him or not, I was so scared.

Then he said, "I am your father, and I am going to take you to your mother and sisters and brothers down in Greenhill, Virginia." When he got me there I found two sisters and four brothers. They was all so glad to see me they shouted and cried and carried on so. I was so scared I tried to run away, because I didn't know nothing about none of them. And I thought that white man what brought me down there ought to have saved me from all this. I just thought a white man was my God, I didn't know no better.

Well, when my folks finally stopped rejoicing my mother only had two chickens. She killed and cooked them for me. My fathers and brothers would go to work every day and leave me at home with my mother for over a year. They would not trust me to work, feared I would run off, because I didn't know nothing about them. Hadn't even heard of a mother and father.

My brother and father would work all day and only get one peck of corn or one pound of meat or one quart of molasses for a whole day's work from sunup till sundown. We had to grind that corn for our flour, and got biscuits once a year at Christmas, and then only one biscuit apiece.

After a little better'n a year after I come, the white man told my father to bring his family and move from Greenhill, Virginia, to Patrick County, Virginia, to his big farm, and farm there for him, and he would give him one-half of all he raised for his share.

We went, and did we raise a big crop! He kept his word all right, and we stayed there till the white man died five years later. Then we went to another farm. We had cleared enough in the five years to buy us a fine pair of oxen and had money besides. We made our crop with a hoe and made good.

Then I left home and run about all over, learned how to play a violin and made my living with it for a long time. I quit that and railroaded about eight years, working on sections and new grading. Then went to Decatur, Alabama, and worked with a land company putting down pipings about three months. I quit that and married Anna Johnson and come to Giles County, Tennessee. We had one son.

I came to St. Louis from Tennessee more than forty years ago. I landscaped out here for sixteen years until I was [too] disabled to work hard any more. I got a garden but I can't make any money from it, because all the other folks out here got gardens, too. I've buried two wives from this very house. I am now living with my third wife, and she is a mighty fine woman.

I am a deacon in Mount Zion Baptist Church right here at the corner. Rev. Thomas is my pastor.

I think these twentieth-century white folks that have principle are trying to make amends to Negroes, to make up for the meanness their foreparents done to us, so I try to forgive them all in my heart for the sake of a few good ones now.

Martha Ziegler

Judged to be over 90 years
when interviewed May 27, 1940,
by Essie W. Smith.

No'm, don't nobody know just how old I is. I was owned by Marse Tom Ziegler, down at Union Hall, in the time before the war. The book where he kept the dates of his niggers was lost after he died, and didn't none of them remember how old they was.

I was a good big gal enduring the civilized war, and kept the flies off Marse Tom's son Jim when he come home from the war with the typhoid fever. Folks didn't have no screens in them days and flies was powerful bothersome to sick folks.

Mr. Jim, he got well and went on back to the war, but two of the other boys was killed and brought home. They was buried in the back of the garden, and you can see their graves there now, if them folks that lives there ain't plowed the graves under. Another of the boys didn't come home, and they ain't never knowed what become of him.

Well, I stayed on there after the niggers was freed. I didn't see no use in making such a fuss over being free. I got to work for my living just the same, and I never could make as much as Marse Tom and his family done give me all the time.

I was right there when him and old Mistess both died. They didn't live so long after the war, and then the chilluns, what was left, married and went away, and the old house was closed for a long time.

A young doctor come to the place about that time, the first one ever to live in that community, and he rented him a house to keep, what he called Bachelor Hall, and I got the place to cook for him. I was about grown then, spry and a tolerable good cook, so he hired me right off. I stayed with him, and when he got married and brought his wife home I just kept right on doing for them.

She was a right likely lady he married, with pretty, long, slick black hair and snapping black eyes, and I lived with them and we got on fine. I helped born all the chilluns and nursed them and looked after things, and helped them save till they accumulated a lot and decided to move to town, where they could send the chilluns to free school that had come in about this time. I come with them, and helped keep things stylish like they had to be, to keep up with the town folks.

The doctor, he died before he was fifty with the pneumonia. He was took sudden and didn't live no time, and I just kept on staying with the widow and doing like I always had done. When the chilluns was right smart size she took and got married again, and the man she picked allowed they could do better in a place a long way off, and they packed up to go.

They wanted me to go along, but I ain't never felt no man fitten to take the doctor's place, and I thinks I better off here where I done know everybody, so I went to the doctor's sister, Miss Ella, who had done got married and was living in the same town, and told her just how I felt.

She didn't like the man no better than I did, and she told me she had to have a new cook as hers was going away, and I could just come on and live with her. She knowed how I had always took care of her brother, and she knowed I would do the same by her.

Her old man was always a good provider, and he was accumulating a lot even in them early days, and she was helping him by being saving and making things go a long ways. They ain't never had no chilluns of their own, but they was always doing for her nieces and nephews like they was theirs.

They was powerful hands for preaching and preachers, too, and there wasn't no Sunday they didn't go to Sunday School and teach there, too. They sent missionaries to foreign countries and done plenty of things for people that nobody didn't know nothing about but me, on account of me hearing them talk while they was eating.

When I begun to get sort of feeble they took me to doctors and specialists everywhere. They done all they could for my eyes, but spite of all the money spent I can't see much now.

They got hands in to help me when I needed them. First they got a girl, in the wood-stove days, to bring in wood and keep the fires going while I was cooking, and then they got a woman to do all the cleaning and the heavy work, and now they done got a man to wait on the table and drive the big car they done bought.

I just keep on getting more and more no-account. They built a house for me in the back yard long time ago, and now they done got a woman to stay there with me, and hand me things, and do for me like I been doing for other folks all my life. They are that good to me, I can't tell you about it all.

But sorrow done come on this house, for Miss Ella's husband, he died here last week. And what do you think? He done left me four thousand dollars! It says so in his will; they had something done to it so as it can't be broke. I am to have every cent that four thousand brings in long as I live, and when I die it goes to an orphanage. He sure was one good man, if he was sometimes testy and always particular and wanting things done just so.

No'm, I wasn't never set on marrying. Them as I liked when I was young mostly choosed somebody else, and them as wanted me I wouldn't have, and then when I went to work for Doctor's family I got so busy I didn't have no time to think about such things, and I ain't had no time, nor inclination, since.

I ain't never been nowhere much and ain't had no desire to travel. When Miss Ella and her old man was taking all them trips, going all over the world, I was that glad I had a place to stay right here taking care of their things, and I didn't have to be going on them ships and being where you couldn't see nothing but water no matter which way you looked. Once I went to see some of my kin in West Virginia, but I done lived like white folks so long I can't endure niggers' ways, and I didn't stay long there, and I ain't wanted to go back since.

I done been a church member all these long years. I 'fessed religion when I was a right young woman, when a revival was going on down there where I lived then. Lots of folks that gets religion these days come to the mourners' bench, and there is shouting and all kinds of goings-on that you don't know nothing about.

I done got right with the Lord, and I am ready to go any time He calls me. I'm ready to stay here long as He wants me to, because I done fell in good hands, but all the same I'm waiting to go. The Lord knows I done the best I could with whatever come to hand, and I'm trusting the rest to Him.

Jane Pyatt

Age 89 when interviewed
by Thelma Dunston in Portsmouth
at 1124 High Street.

Mrs. Pyatt was born in Middlesex County.
At only three months of age,
she was sold with her mother to
a Norfolk slaveholder who shortly
moved to Portsmouth.

During slavery there weren't any schools for slaves or free Negroes in this city. Some of the slave owners taught their slaves the right from the wrong, while others didn't. The real character of a slave was brought out by the respect they had for each other. Most of the time there was no force back of the respect the slaves had for each other, and yet they were for the most part truthful, loving, and respectful to one another.

When I was growing up, although I was a slave, I had everything a person could wish for except an education. I worked in the house with my mistress, and I was able to learn lots from her. Although it was against the law to teach a slave my mistress taught me my alphabets. By listening to my mistress talk I learned how to use a lot of words correctly. I can't write or spell, but strange as it sounds I can read anything I wish. Sometimes I believe my ability to read is a gift from God.

Previous to 1861, there weren't any policemen, but there were patrollers instead. Their duty was the same as that of the policemen of today. If the slaves had a corn-shucking party or a prayer meeting, and if they made too much noise, the patrollers would arrest them.

When slaves visited they were given passes, and the patrollers would inspect all visiting slaves to see if they had a pass with them. If they did not have a pass they were locked up. Sometimes the officials would beat them, and sometimes they would sell them. These patrollers took two of my brothers, one seven years old and the other one five years old, and I have never seen either since. Where they were carried, none of our family has ever been able to find out.

On North Street, in the same block that the Emanuel A.M.E. Church stands today, there was an old brick building. The cellar of the building led into an underground railroad. This passageway extended to the ferry of the Elizabeth River. Boats stayed there all the time, making it possible for many slaves to escape. Men, women, and children would pack their clothes during the day and escape at night through this underground railroad.

In 1861 the Yankees took Portsmouth. When the Yankees marched through the city the slaves fell in line and followed the Union Army. It was in that year that we had our first Negro policemen, Chief of Police, and Justice of

Peace. Mr. John Wilson was the first Negro Chief of Police, and Mr. Thomas Davis was the first Negro Justice of Peace.

In 1861 the Seaboard Railroad was on High Street, and boxcars stayed on three blocks of this street all of the time. The Yankees would get near these boxcars and play music, and the slaves would gather around to hear the music. Then the Yankees would fill the boxcars with slaves, and take them away.

The harbors at Portsmouth was blockaded in 1861. At this time the Yankees entered the Norfolk Navy Yard and took ships that they wanted, and the ships they didn't want, they burned. The *Pennsylvania* was one of the ships that was burned by the Yankees. When there were guns on the burning ships they were left there. When the guns got hot they would explode, completely destroying the ships. The Confederate Army took the hull of one of the burnt ships and built the *Merrimac*. During this year Portsmouth was evacuated. Many people fled farther south for fear that the city would be burned.

In 1866 a mayor was elected head of the city, and the colored policemen, Justice of Peace, and Chief of Police were done away with. In their places a provost marshal with a white staff was appointed.

Luke D. Dixon

Age 81 when interviewed
by Irene Robertson at
De Valls Bluff, Arkansas.

To Dixon's narrative, Ms. Robertson
adds the following note:
"This Negro is well-fixed for living
at home. He is large and very black,
but his wife is a light mulatto with curly,
nearly straightened hair. On the wall
in the dining room, used as a sitting
room, was a framed picture of
Booker T. Washington and Teddy Roosevelt
sitting at a round-shaped hotel dining table
ready to be served. Underneath the picture
in large print was *EQUALITY*."

My father's owner was Jim Dixon in Elmo County, Virginia. Not far from Richmond. That is where I was born. Ma belong to Harper Williams. We lived on the big road that run to the Atlantic Ocean. Ma lived three or four miles from Pa. She lived across Big Creek—now they call it Farroh's Run. Pa's folks was very good but Ma's folks was unpleasant.

The white folks had an iron clip that fastened the thumbs

together, and they would swing the man or woman up in a tree and whip them. I seen that done in Virginia across from where I lived. I don't know what the folks had done. They pulled the man up with block and tackle.

Another thing I seen done was put three or four chinquapin switches together green, twist them, and dry them. They would dry like a leather whip. They whipped the slaves with them.

I used to set on Grandma's lap and she told me about how they used to catch people in Africa. She said some they captured, they left bound till they come back, and sometimes they never went back to get them. They died.

They herded them up like cattle and put them in stalls and brought them on the ship and sold them. They had room in the stalls on the boat to set down or lie down. They put several together. Put the men to themselves and the women to themselves.

When a boat was to come in, people come and wait to buy slaves. They had several days of selling. I never seen this but that is the way it was told to me. When they sold Grandma and Grandpa at a fishing dock called Newport, Virginia, they had their feet bound down and their hands bound crossed, up on a platform.

Grandpa was named Sam Abraham, and Phillis Abraham was his mate. They was sold twice. Once she was sold away from her husband to a speculator.

Well, it was hard on the Africans to be treated like cattle. They sold Grandma's daughter to somebody in Texas. She cried and begged to let them be together. They didn't pay no attention to her. She couldn't talk [English] but she made them know she didn't wanted to be parted. Six years after slavery they got together.

I have heard of slaves buying their own freedom. I don't know how it was done. I have heard of folks being helped to run off. Grandma on Mother's side had a brother run off from Dalton, Mississippi, to the North. After the war he come to Virginia.

The Ku Klux was bad. They took the place of pattyrollers before freedom. They was a band of land owners what took the law in hand. I scared to be caught out.

Jim Dixon had several boys—Baldwin and Joe. Joe took some of the slaves his pa give him and went to New Mexico to shun the war. Uncle and Pa went in the war as waiters. They went in at the ending-up. My father got his leg shot off.

Dixon never told us we was free, but at the end of the year he gave my father a gray mule he had ploughed for a long time and part of the crop. My mother just picked us up and left her folks now. She was cooking then, I recollect. Folks just went wild when they got turned loose.

My parents was first married under a twenty-five-cents license law in Virginia. After freedom they was remarried under a new law and the license cost more, but I forgot how much. You could register under any name you give yourself. My father went by the name of Right Dixon and Mother, Jilly Dixon. They had fourteen children to my knowing.

When freedom was declared we left and went to

Wilmington and Wilson, North Carolina. Ma lived to be 103 years old. Pa died in 1905, and was 105 years old. I never went to public school but two days in my life. I went to night school and paid Mr. J. C. Price and Mr. S. H. Vick to teach me.

I come to Arkansas, brought my wife and one child, April 5, 1889. Her people come from North Carolina and Moultrie, Georgia. I had to work. It kept me out of meanness. Work and that woman has kept me right.

I do vote. I vote a Republican ticket. I sell eggs or a little something and keep my taxes paid up. It looks like I'm the kind of folks the government would help—them that works and tries hard to have something—but seems like they don't get no help. They wouldn't help me if I was about to starve.

Candis Goodwin

Age about 80
when interviewed at Cape Charles.

I ain't knowed, exactly, how old I is, but I born before the war. Born over yonder at Seaview, on old Massa Scott's plantation. It ain't far from here.

My mommer, she work in the quarter-kitchen. She ain't have to work hard like some. What about my pappy? Well, you know, Uncle Stephen, he kind of overseer for some widow womans—he Mommer's husband. He come see my mommer any time he gets ready. But I find out he ain't my pappy.

I knowed that since when I was a little thing. I used to go over to Massa Williams' plantation. The folks over there, they used to say to me, "Who's your pappy? Who's your pappy?" I just say, "Turkey buzzard lay me and the sun hatch me," and then go on about my business.

'Course all the time they know and I know, too, that Massa Williams was my pappy. I tell you something else.

Got a brother living right on this here street. But it ain't knowed round here. It would ruin him. 'Course he's white. One of them tooth doctors, you know, what pulls your teeth.

My white people, they good to me. Never had no work to do in them days, excepting nursing the babies. Used to go over to Nottinghams' to play, go 'long with Missus's chillun, you know. I like to go over there, because they has good jam and biscuits. If they don't give me none I just take some. They don't do nothing, just say, "Take your hand out that plate." But I got what I wants then.

Sh! We chillun used to have a time around old Missus's place. All us chillun used to get together and go in the woods to play. The great big white boys used to go 'long with us, too. We take the brown pine shadows [needles] and make houses out of them and then make grass out of the green ones. Then we go over Missus's dairy and steal anything we want and take it to our houses in the woods. Them was good old times, I tell you, honey.

Tell you what I used to do. I used to play pranks on old Massa Scott. I was regular little devil, I was. Come night, everybody sit around big fireplace in living room. Soon it get kind of late, Massa get up out of his chair to wind up the clock. I get behind his chair right easy, and quick sneak his chair from under him, and when he finish, he set smack on the floor! Then he say, "Doggone, you little cattin, I gone switch you!" I just fly out of the room. Wasn't scared, though, because I know Massa wasn't gone do nothing to me.

What I know about whipping? Massa Scott never had none of that kind of stuff on his place. He say it ain't right. He didn't never strike one of his niggers; nobody else better not, neither. Didn't allow no pattyrollers around. Say they treacherous. Massa Nottingham never had them on his place, neither.

Honey, I tell you I growed just as good as any child in this country. Old Missus Scott give me good clothes; 'course I didn't get them more than twice a year, but they's good when I gets them. She give me Sis's dresses. Sis one of Missus's little girls.

And the white chillun, they learn me how to read, too. 'Course the white folks didn't want you to learn. I remember just as clear as yesterday how one of them chillun learn me how to read *compress-i-bility*. Thought I was something, then! I can read Bible little now, but I can't write; never learn to write.

Did I ever go to church? 'Course I did! Went right along with Missus's chillun. Had to set in the back, but that wasn't nothing. Sometimes the old folk used to get together in the quarter-kitchen to shout and pray. That's where my mommer get religion. She kind of tender woman, couldn't stand that preaching no longer.

Yes, they had overseers. Had colored ones, too. Massa Scott had white overseers, but Massa Nottingham, he had big black boss on his place, can't remember his name. He ain't had to get no permission to come to our place. He just come and goes when he gets ready.

Can I remember the war? Yes, indeed! Remember just

like it was yesterday. Yes, reckon I about six year old when the Yankees come—just a little thing, you know. Well, they had a store down the corner from Massa's plantation, and they always send me to store for to buy things. Used to go down there and them Yankees be sitting all along the road with they blue coats, right pretty sight, it was. But I was scared to death, when I gets near them. I gets what I wants from the store and flies past them.

Them Yankees sure had they way. They went in all the white folks' house; take they silver and anything they big enough carry out. Just ruin Missus's furniture; get up on the table and just cut caper. Nasty things!

Then the Yankees goes round at night, take anybody they wants to help them fight. Got my Jake; 'course I never knowed him then. He twelve year older I is.

Let me tell you about my Jake, how he did in the war. He big man in the war. He drill soldiers every day. First he be in one them companies—Company C, I believe. Then he worked up to be sergeant major, in the Tenth Regiment. Jacob Goodwin, his name was. He say all look up to him and respect him, too. See that sword over in that corner? That's the very sword he used in the war, and I kept it all these years. No, the soldiers never did no fighting round here as I know of. But plenty of them camped here.

My Jake, he handsome man, he was. Remember how we first got together. We all was to church one Sunday, and Jake, he kept sidling up to me. And I looking at him out of the corner of my eye, till finally he come up and took hold of my hands. I was in my early teens then. It was after the war; I had growed up. They say I was the prettiest girl on the Shore. And when Jake and me got married everybody said, "You sure make a pretty couple."

The old Scott chillun what I growed up with, none them left now. They last girl died last year, and her daughter come way down here from up in Maryland to tell Aunt Candis about it. Wouldn't tell me, scared it would excite me. But I heard her telling my child there all about it. They's all mighty nice folks, them Scotts is. Some them, they still comes to see me. Slip me some money now and then, and something to eat, too.

Levi Pollard

Age 88 when interviewed
on Clark Street in Richmond.

I think I was born June 30, round eighty-eight years ago, on Marse Charles Bruce's plantation in Charlotte County, Virginia.

Marse Charles was a powerful rich man, come into two millions dollars when he was born a baby. He son were good to us niggers; he ain't work us hard, that he ain't.

My pappy and mammy live on his place. Pappy, he haul every day with the wagon. Mammy, she make clothes for the white folks, and for the niggers, too. She go to the big house every Monday and gets the things they wants make and tote them home, cut them out, make them, and tote them back all done before that next Monday. Then she had the knitting, and sometimes spinning with the spinning wheel.

Aunt Becky and Aunt Ellen was sewers like Mammy.

They was all sisters, and when they was small old Miss—that Marse Charles's ma—learn them to sew. They say she was some kind of good to the niggers.

Us had us a two-story-high house and only us lived there. I mean, no other folks lived there, even to Aunt Becky and Aunt Ellen. They was two rooms downstairs, one the kitchen, and Mammy and Pappy and the other chillun sleep in that other room, and in the kitchen, too. They was fourteen chilluns in all.

Upstairs, you could stand up in the middle and on the sides you can't, because the roof cuts the sides off. But part of the chillun stay up there. Some sleep in the corner, and if they disremember that the top were close by they ain't disremember long, because they head would sure get a swelled egg on it. I done got many a egg; wonder it ain't cracked good fashion right now.

There was other things in the house—beds and pallets, and benches what they use for prayer meetings, and any of the white folks's throw-offs. The kitchen had a high fireplace in it. That where us cook.

Us had right smart rations. Cornbread was make up for ashcakes; they was baked in the fireplace. When the ashes was hot, you just push the pone that you had patted out with your fingers in them ashes and let it get done, then you pull it out and wash it off, and scrape it so as it was clean, and then eat it. They was mighty good.

Meat from the smokehouse was gived us every four week. Us get twelve pounds, and that had to last on us;

ain't get no more. Side and shoulder of the hog, cured and put down in plenty of salt. Us always have that for dinner. Cut it up in square pieces and let it boil, then put in your salad, or cabbages, or beans, and they was some kind of good.

Marse had 180 cows, so us had all the milk us could drink. They was peach trees and apple trees that us could have for usself. Us had watermelons and mushmelons also. Marse had pear trees that he said nobody couldn't eat; they was for the house. But I had many of them. I climb the tree at night and eat them up there.

Here the way us eat in slavery. Us eat breakfast round eight o'clock. The folks that was in the fields would come home, or else the ones at home would tote it to them. They go to work round five and six o'clock. They ain't eat before they go. Us eat mush and things like that for breakfast.

Dinner was half past twelve or one o'clock. Always nearly have boil dinner, or fried dinner, or soup.

For supper most times molasses and cornbread, or hind and milk, or suppers something like that. This was round six o'clock.

On Sunday evenings us have a man named Dr. Beale Bassette, that Marse bought from some Quaker people. He was a preacher, and on Sunday evenings he open his house for the niggers' chillun to come get education.

He have Sunday School, where he read the Bible and pray. This here us used to sing on Sunday at school:

When I done been redeemed and done been tried,

I'll sit down beside the lamb.

Can't you read? Can't you read?

When I done been to heaven then,

I can read my title clean.

When I done been to heaven,

I's going to get my lesson,

I's going to read,

I's going to read my title clean.

Then he use the *New York Primer*, with great big letters in it. He show us how to make them, and us was learning good when Missy Smith take our books.

Missy Nannie Smith live at the big house, but she ain't like niggers like Marse's folks do. One Sunday she come to Sunday School with a big pile of cakes. They was colored up as pretty as a picture. She say, "You niggers come get good cake," and when us see it, eyes pop clean out of our heads, because Missy Smith, she ain't never been that good before, nor since neither.

She keep calling for us to come get the cakes, and then our bellies start calling for the cake. Us ain't never had bread made up with flour, let alone cake with flour and sugar in it. One nigger got up and run to her, and she gived the cake, then she say, "Let me see your primer."

She taken the book, but the nigger had the pretty, big cake. Then all us run up to her and get the cake us wants so bad. Soon the cakes was gone and so was our books.

She say, "I don't want you niggers to learn how to read and write; niggers ain't got no right to know."

After that I stop going on Sunday nights, because the very thing that I want, I ain't get. I ain't never been to no school after then. Missy Nannie teach us this here poetry the time she take us books:

One drop of water
And a cool grain of sand
Makes the highest ocean,
All round the beautiful land.

She say this was education, but it ain't learn me to read, and it ain't learn me to write, and it ain't learn me to count. I don't know what it is learn me to do.

I had a cousin Paul that had some learning. He got his from his marse when he drive him places. He learn me how to count by ones, and by five, and by ten, to one hundred. Listen: 1-2-3-4-5-6-7-8-9-8. I get mixed up there all the time, but I always remember after that: 10 comes after 9.

Now, I can count up to one hundred by five: 5-10-15-20-25- . . . Is you writing as I count? I can do that good as anybody can. I can count money good, too. I ain't never been cheated, as far as I know of.

There was a church on Marse Charles's plantation that the niggers used to go and sit in the gallery. They was a white preacher, and the white folks sit downstairs.

Niggers have benches in they house that they use when

they have prayer meetings. When they have it at our house they take and sit the beds outside and put the benches like in the church. They always has a watcher to look out for pattyrollers. They turn a pot down so as not to let the sound go far. [It was an ancient African practice to invert a large cooking or wash pot in the belief that it would capture secret conversations.]

In the summer or on holidays us can go a-visiting to Marse Jim or Marse Dick, or to Missy Clark. They was Marse Charles's brothers and sister. If the holiday fall on Saturday us go Friday night and come back Sunday afternoon. In summertime us can stay as long as two weeks visiting.

Christmastime, Marse Charles gived us lots of things. Sometimes they would be a little extra, but us always got a peck of flour, a whole ham, five pounds real cane sugar, and everybody winter clothes. Every man gets two working shirts, one coat, one pair pants, one jacket, and one pair shoes. The women get near about the same, I reckon; I ain't never been good at remembering things I ain't knowed nothing about, and I ain't never been married.

The way they marry on Marse Charles's plantation was like this—'course I ain't never been hanked up, but I seen a heap of them. First you pick out the gal you want, then ask her to marry up with you, then go to Marse and ask him if you can have her. If Marse like that couple then he say yes, and he go and get the house for them to live in on the plantation. Then they is ready for the big day.

Maybe the bride marry in her house, and maybe she

marry in some other nigger's house. I heard tell of some niggers marrying in they marse's house, but I ain't seed none of that. I ain't saying it's true, and I ain't saying it's not true.

The bride dresses all up in white with a pretty veil. Where she get the veil? The white folks must gived it to her, or some of the niggers that was married up before must let her have theirs. I reckon many a one taken the curtains from the windows and use them.

Her best girl friends would be her maids, and they would all get round her to keep her all right till it was all over. The maids was dressed fit to kill. Some of them look like they had on everything that they saw in the house, like tablecloths and curtains and counterpanes, and everything else they think make them look good. One thing sure, they ain't use all this here red paint like the gals uses nowdays, and they ain't go about burning up they hair God give them, like the gals and old women does this here times.

The groom would dress in his best Sunday clothes. It must be that Marse gived him one of his old clothes for that special. Marse Charles say he give me a fine suit if I married, but I ain't never got that fine suit up to now, and Marse Charles is been dead so long that I know I ain't never going get it. The groom's mens wore the best they had. They duty was to look after him till he got hanked up.

Sometimes the white folks come to see them marry off. It all depend on who was marrying.

At the time that was set old Dr. Beale Bassette would

stand up and clear his throat, and call them to order. Then the bride and her maids march down the aisle to where he is, and then the groom and his mens march down to where she is, and there they stand. Dr. Bassette read to them, and then the bride and groom take hands, and they was fixed.

After that they have the reception. That was where us kicked up fun. They mostly have banjo for music. Everybody sing and clap the hands and dance and have one good time, just the same as us was white folks.

When a feller comes a-knocking they holler, Oh, sho'!
Hop light, ladies, oh, Miss Loo.
Oh, swing that yaller gal, do, boys, do,
Hop light, ladies, oh, Miss Loo.

Look at that mulatto man, a-follering up Sue,
Hop light, ladies, oh, Miss Loo.
The boys ain't a-going when you cry boo-hoo,
Hop light, ladies, oh, Miss Loo.

The bride and groom be there having they good time. They always joke them after the wedding. The old folks say, "When you-all gonna leave this here reception and go to bed?"

They get right smart 'shame, but they laugh; but timely everybody notice that the bride and groom was going, and then they put that down to tease them, sure's you born.

Law, what kind of work I done in slavery? First thing I

do was mind the cows, me and two slave boys. I ain't do that long, 'cause they put me to toting water to the hands in the fields. I was strong then, let alone what I is now, even though I don't look like it.

I ain't know there was no war near, but I seed funny things. The white folks was all sad and a-crying, and they ain't bother the niggers a-tall.

Then one day the overseer say, "Levi, you know there is war going on, and the niggers that was plowing is gone off to help us win the war. You has made yourself honorable; you is going have a trustworthy job."

He say, "You is not ripe enough to go; stay here and work hard so as us can feed the men at war, and so as us can look after the women folks and the young."

I say I do the best I can.

I plowed all that year, then the next fall I gets me two horses to plow with, and then after that I ain't never seed that bucket no more that I toted before. I even plow part in the day Lee surrendered.

Marse Charles ain't go to war; he was older for it. He come and tell all the niggers they was free just as soon as he find out hisself.

That day us go to our house and just clap our hands and sing and dance, and thank the Lord that us is free. Us sure was happy, though I don't reckon us had no right to be, since us was most like white folks. Marse ain't treat us like us was real slaves, like lots of niggers was treated.

Marse Charles say that us ain't belong to him no more,

but that if us want to stay, then he would pay us money to work for him.

Some of the niggers leave when they learn they can go, but us stay where us was born and bred, and live in the same fine house and do the same kind of work; but us get real money for it—a hundred dollars a year. Then us was our own boss, and could come and go like any white. And on top of that us could have crops and a garden round the house, sure's you born.

Fannie Berry

Age unknown.
Interviewed February 20, 1937,
in Petersburg by Susie Byrd.

At the Battle of the Crater,
referred to below, a Union regiment
tunneled under the Confederate line
during the siege of Petersburg and
detonated four tons of black powder.
The blast left a crater 170 feet wide
and 30 feet deep.

Back before the sixties, I can remember my mistress, Miss Sara Ann, coming to the window and hollering, "The niggers is a-rising! The niggers is a-rising! The niggers is killing all the white folks, killing all the babies in the cradle!" It must have been Nat Turner's Insurrection, which was sometime before the breaking of the Civil War.

I was waiting on table in dining room, and this day they had finished eating early, and I was cleaning off table. Don't you know I must have been a good-size gal.

This is the song I heard my master sing:

Old John Brown came to Harper's Ferry Town,
Purpose to raise an insurrection;
Old Governor Wise put the specs upon his eyes
And showed him the happy land of Canaan.

Yes, I remember something about him [John Brown], too. I know my master came home and said that on his way to the gallows, old John stopped and kissed a little nigger child. How come I don't remember? Don't tell me I don't, because I do. I don't care if it's done been a thousand years. I know what Master said, and it is as fresh in my mind as it was that day.

Now, Miss Sue, take up. I just like to talk to you about them days of slavery, because you look like you want to hear all about them. But oh, honey, some slaves would be beat up so, when they resisted; and sometimes if you rebelled the overseer would kill you. Us colored women had to go through a-plenty, I tell you.

I was one slave that the poor white man had his match. One tried to throw me, but he couldn't. We tussled and knocked over chairs, and when I got a grip I scratched his face all to pieces; and there was no more bothering Fannie from him.

Yes, I can recollect the blowing up of the Crater. We had fled, but I do know about the shelling of Petersburg. We left Petersburg when the shelling commenced and went to Pamplin in boxcars, getting out of the way. Them were scared times, too, because you looked to be killed any minute by stray bullets.

Just before the shelling of Petersburg they were selling little niggers for little nothing, hardly. Junius Broadie, a white man, bought some niggers, but they didn't stay slave long, because the Yankees came and set them free.

I was at Pamplin and the Yankees and Rebels were fighting, and they were waving the bloody flag, and a Confederate soldier was upon a post, and they were shooting terribly. Guns were firing everywhere.

All a-sudden they struck up "Yankee Doodle" song. A soldier came along and called to me, "How far is it to the Rebels?" and honey, I was feared to tell him. So I said, "I don't know."

He called me again. Scared to death, I was. I recollect getting behind the house and pointed in the direction. You see, if the Rebels knew that I told the soldier they would have killed me.

These were the Union men going after Lee's army, which had done been before them to Appomattox.

The Colored regiment came up behind, and when they saw the Colored regiment they put up the white flag— you remember, before this red or bloody flag was up. Now, do you know why they raised that white flag? Well, honey, that white flag was a token that Lee had surrendered.

Glory! Glory! Yes, child, the Negroes are free, and when they know that they were free, oh, baby, began to sing:

Mammy, don't you cook no more,
You are free, you are free.
Rooster, don't you crow no more,

You are free, you are free.
Old hen, don't you lay no more eggs,
You free, you free.

Such rejoicing and shouting, you never heard in your life. Child, and here's another one we used to sing. Remember, the war done been when we could sing these songs. Listen, now:

Ain't no more blowing of that before-day horn—
I will sing, brethren, I will sing.
A cold, frosty morning the nigger's mighty good,
Take your ax upon your shoulder.
Nigger, talk to the woods.
Ain't no more blowing of that before-day horn—
I will sing, brethren, I will sing.

But poor things, they had no place to go after they got freed. Baby, all us was helpless and ain't had nothing. I was free a long time before I knew it. My mistress still hired me out, till one day in talking to the woman she hired me to, she said, "Fannie, you are free, and I don't have to pay your master for you now. You stay with me." She didn't give me no money, but let me stay there and work for vittles and clothes, because I ain't had nowhere to go.

Jesus, Jesus, God help us! You chillun don't know. I didn't say nothing when she was telling me, but done decided to leave her and go back to the white folks that first owned me. And do you know, I didn't leave that woman's house no more for fifteen years!

Elder Williams married me in Miss Delia Mann's parlor on the Crater road. The house still stands. The house was full of colored people. Miss Sue Jones and Miss Molley Clark waited on me. They took the lamps and we walked up to the preacher. One waiter joined my hand and one my husband's hand.

After marriage the white folks give me a reception; and honey, talking about a table—it was stretched clean across the dining room.

We had everything to eat you could call for. No, didn't have no common eats. We could sing in there, and dance old square dance all us choosed. Lord, Lord! I can see them gals now on that floor, just skipping and a-trotting. And honey, there was no white folks to set down and eat before you.

Richard Slaughter

Age nearly 88 when interviewed
by Claude S. Anderson
on December 27, 1936, at Hampton.

I was born a slave. My owner's name was Dr. Epps. I was born January 9, 1849, on the James at a place called Epps Island, City Point. I stayed there until I was around thirteen or fourteen years old, when I came to Hampton. How old am I? Well, there's the date. Count it up for yourself. Did slaves ever run away? Lord, yes. All the time. Where I was born there is a lots of water. Why, there used to be as high as ten and twelve Dutch three-masters in the harbor at a time. In those days a good captain would hide a slave way up in the topsail and carry him out of Virginia to New York and Boston. I used to catch little snakes and other things like terrapins and sell them to the sailors for to eat roaches on the ships.

I don't know much about the meanness of slavery. There was so many degrees in slavery, and I belonged to a very nice man. He never sold but one man, far's I can remember, and that was Cousin Ben. Sold him south. Yes. My master was a nice old man. He ain't living now. Dr. Epps died and his son wrote me my age. I got it upstairs in a letter now.

When McClellan retreated from Richmond through the peninsula to Washington, I came to Hampton as a government water boy. Hampton was already burnt when I came here. I came to Hampton in June 1862. When I first came to Hampton there were only barracks where the Institute is; when I returned General Armstrong had done right smart.

The Yankees burned Hampton and the fleet went up the James River. The gunboats would fire on the towns and plantations and run the white folks off. After that they would carry all the colored folks back down here to Old Point and put them behind the Union lines. My father and mother and cousins went aboard the *Meritanza* with me. You see, my father and three or four men left in the darkness first and got aboard.

While I was aboard the gunboat she captured a Rebel gunboat at a place called Drury's Bluff. I know the names of all the gunboats that came up the river. Yessir. There was the *Galena*—we called her "the old cheese box"—the *Delaware*, the *Yankee*, the *Hooker*, and the *Meritanza*, which was the ship I was board of. I had the measles on the *Meritanza* and was put off at Harrison's Landing.

I left Hampton still working as a water boy and went to Quire Creek, Bell Plains, Virginia, a place near Harper's Ferry. I left the creek aboard a steamer, the *General Hooker*, and went to Alexandria, Virginia. Abraham Lincoln came aboard the steamer and we carried him to Mount Vernon, George Washington's old home. What did he look like? Why, he looked more like an old preacher than anything I know. Heh! Heh! Heh! Have you ever seen any pictures of him? Well, if you seen a picture of him you seen him. He's just like the picture.

You say you think I speak very good English. Well, son, I ought to. I been everywhere. No, I never went to what you would call school, except to school as a soldier. I went to Baltimore in 1864 and enlisted. I was about seventeen years old then.

I was assigned to the Nineteenth Regiment of Maryland Company B. My officers' names were Captain Joe Reed, Lieutenant Stimson, and Colonel Joseph E. Perkins. While I was in training they fought at Petersburg. I went to the regiment in '64 and stayed in until '67. I was a cook. They taken Richmond the fifth day of April, 1865.

I have never been wounded. My clothes have been cut off me by bullets, but the Lord kept them off my back, I guess.

When we left Richmond my brigade was ordered to Brownsville, Texas. We went there by way of Old Point Comfort, where we went aboard a transport. When we got to Brownsville I was detailed to a hospital staff. We arrived in Brownsville in January 1867.

The only thing that happened in Brownsville while I was there was the hanging of three Mexicans for the murder of an aide. In September we left Brownsville and came back to Baltimore. I then returned to Hampton and lived as an oysterman and fisherman for over forty years.

While I was away my father died in Hampton. He waited on an officer. My mother lived in Hampton and saw me married in 1874. I bought a lot on Union Street for a hundred dollars cash. I reared a nephew, gave him the lot and the house I built on it, and he threw it away. When I moved around here I paid cash for this house.

During the World War, I went to Washington and haven't been anyplace since. I'm a little hard of hearing and have high blood pressure. So I have to sit most of the time. Got an invitation in there now wanting me to come to a grand reunion of Yankees and the Rebels this year, but I can't go. Getting too old.

Sara Colquitt

Age estimated at 100-plus
when interviewed by Preston Klein
September 9, 1937, at Opelika, Alabama.

Colquitt relates her experience
of slavery first in Richmond,
where she was born, and later,
briefly, in Alabama, where she
was taken after being sold.

Mr. Bill Slaughter and Miss Mary Slaughter was our marsa and mistess, and they had two chilluns, Marsa Robert and Marsa Brat. Us lived in log cabins with dirt floors, and they was built in two long rows. Us beds was nailed to the wall at one end, and us used corn shucks and pine straw for mattresses.

Us cooked on a great big fireplace what had arms hanging out over the coals to hang pots on to boil. Then us had three-legged skillets what set right over the coals for frying and such like. Us cooked sure-'nuff bread in them days—ashcakes, the best thing you ever et. They ain't nothing like that these days.

Miss Mary was good to us, but us had to work hard and late. I worked in the fields every day from before daylight to almost plumb dark. I used to take my littlest baby with me, and I'd tie it up to a tree limb to keep off the ants and bugs whilst I hoed and worked the furrow.

Let me see, who I married? I mighty nigh forgot who it was I did marry. Now I knows. It was Prince Hodnett. I had two chilluns. They was named Lou and Eli, and they was took care of like the rest.

I was one of the spinners, too, and had to do six cuts to the reel at the time, and do it at night plenty times. Us clothes was homespun osnaburg, what us would dye, sometimes solid and sometimes checked.

Besides working the fields and spinning, sometimes I'd help with the cooking up at the big house when the real cook was sick or us had a passel of company.

Us used to have some good times. Us could have all the fun us wanted on Saturday nights, and us sure had it, cutting monkeyshines and dancing all night long sometimes. Sometimes our mistess would come down early to watch us dance. Some would pat and sing,

> Keys not a-running,
> Keys not a-running.

And us sure did more than dance, I'm telling you.

Next to our dances the most fun was corn shucking. Marster would have the corn hauled up to the cribs and piled as [high as] a house. Then he would invite the hands around to come and help shuck it.

Us had two leaders or generals and choose up two sides. Then us see which side would win first, and holler and sing. I disremembers the hollers just now. My mind is sort of missing. Marster would pass the jug around, too. Then they sure could work, and that pile'd just vanish.

Us used the white folks' church in the morning. I joined the church then, because I always tried to live right and with the Lord.

I was sold once before I left Virginia. Then I was brung down to Alabama and sold from the block for a thousand dollars to Mr. Sam Rainey, at Camp Hill, Alabama. I still worked in the fields, but I would cook for the white folks and help around the big house on special occasions. I used to stop by the spring house to get the milk—it was good cold, too—and tote it up to the big house for dinner.

Our overseer was Mr. Green Ross, and he was a bad one, too. Mean, my goodness! He'd whip you in a minute. He'd put you in the buck, tie your feet, and then set out to whip you right. [In a buck, the wrists were bound, arms hugging knees, with a rod thrust through the angle between arms and knees, thus immobilizing the slave for punishment.]

He would get us slaves up before day, blowing on his big horn, and us would work till plumb dark. All the little niggers'd get up, too, and go up to the big house to be fed from wooden bowls. Then they'd be called again before us come from the fields and put to bed by dark.

No'm, I don't want no more slavery. I hope they don't have no more such, because it was terrible.

Lucinda Elder

Age 86 when interviewed
at 1007 Edward Street
in Houston, Texas.

You chilluns all go way now, while I talks to this gentleman. I declare to goodness, chilluns nowadays ain't got no manners at all. It ain't like when I was little. They learned you manners, and you learned to mind, too. Nowadays you tell them to do something and you is just wasting you breath, unless you has a stick right handy. They is my great-grandchilluns, and they sure is spoilt. Maybe I ain't got no patience no more, like I used to have, because they ain't so bad.

Well, sir, you-all wants me to tell you about slave times, and I'll tell you first that I had mighty good white folks, and I hope they is gone up to heaven. My mama belonged to Marse John Cardwell, what I hear was the richest man and had the biggest plantation round Concord Depot, in Campbell County, in Virginny. I don't remember old

Missy's name, but she mighty good to the slaves, just like Marse John was.

Mama's name was Isabella, and she was the cook, and born right on the plantation. Papa's name was Gibson. His first name was Jim, and he belonged to Marse Gibson, what had a plantation next to Marse John, and I know Papa come to see Mama on Wednesday and Saturday nights.

Let me see now, there was six of us chilluns. My memory ain't so good no more, but Charley was oldest, then come Dolly and Jennie and Susie and me and Laura. Law me, I guess old Dr. Bass, what was doctor for Marse John, used to be right busy with us about once a year for quite a spell.

Them times, they don't marry by no license. They take a slave man and woman from the same plantation and put them together, or sometimes a man from another plantation, like my papa and mama. Mama say Marse John give them a big supper in the big house and read out the Bible about obeying and working, and then they are married. 'Course the nigger just a slave and have to do what the white folks say, so that way of marrying about good as any.

But Marse John sure was the good marse, and we had plenty to eat and wear and no one ever got whipped. Marse say if he have a nigger what ought to be whipped he'd get rid of him quick, because a bad nigger just like a rotten tater in a sack of good ones—it spoil the others.

Back there in Virginny it sure get cold in winter, but come September the wood gang get busy cutting wood and hauling it to the yard. They makes two piles, one for the big house and the biggest pile for the slaves. When they get it all hauled it look like a big wood yard.

While they is hauling the women make quilts, and they is wool quilts. They ain't made out of shearing wool, but just as good. Marse John have lots of sheep, and when they go through the briar patch the wool catch on them briars, and in the fall the women folks goes out and picks the wool off the briars just like you pick cotton. Law me, I don't know nothing about making quilts out of cotton till I come to Texas.

Marse John won't work no one till they is fifteen years old. Then they works three hours a day and that all. They don't work full time till they's eighteen. We was just same as free niggers on our place. He give each slave a piece of ground to make the crop on and buy the stuff hisself. We growed snap beans and corn and plant on a light moon; or turnips and onions we plant on the dark moon.

When I get old enough Marse John let me take his daughter, Nancy Lee, to school. It is twelve miles, and the yard man hitches up old Bess to the buggy and we get in, and no one in that county no prouder than what I was.

Marse John let us go visit other plantations, and no pass, neither. If the pattyroller stop us we just say we belong to Marse John, and they don't bother us none. If they come to our cabin from other plantations they has to show the pattyroller the pass, and if they slipped off and ain't got none the pattyroller sure give a whipping then. But they wait till they off our place, because Marse John won't allow no whipping on our place by no one.

Well, things was just about the same all the time till just before freedom. 'Course I hears some talk about bluebellies—what they call the Yanks—fighting our folks, but they wasn't fighting around us. Then one day Mama took sick, and she had hear talk, and call me to the bed and say, "Lucinda, we all going to be free soon and not work unless we get paid for it."

She sure was right. Marse John call all us to the cookhouse and read the freedom papers to us and tell us we is all free, but if we want to stay he'll give us land to make a crop and he'll feed us. Now, I tell you the truth, they wasn't no one leave, because we all love Marse John.

Then, just three weeks after freedom, Mama dies, and that how come me to leave Marse John. You see, Marse Gibson, what own Papa before freedom, was a good marse, and when Papa was set free Marse Gibson give him some land to farm. 'Course Papa was going to have us all with him, but when Mama dies Marse Gibson tell him Mr. Will Jones and Miss Susie, his wife, want a nurse girl for the chilluns, so Papa hired me out to them. And I want to say right now, they just as good white folks as Marse John and old Missy, and sure treated me good.

I never won't forget one day Mr. Will say, "Lucinda, we is going to drive over to Appomattox and take the chilluns, and you can come, too." I was tickled most to pieces, but he didn't tell what he going for. You know what? To see a nigger hung. I getting along mighty old now, but I won't never forget that. He had killed a man, and I never saw so many people before, there to see him hang. I just shut my eyes.

Then Mr. Will, he take me to the big tree what have all the bark strip off it and the branches strip off and say, "Lucinda, this tree where General Lee surrender." I has put these two hands right on that tree, yessir, I sure has.

Miss Susie say one day, "Lucinda, how you like to go with us to Texas?" Law me, I didn't know where Texas was at or nothing, but I loved Mr. Will and Miss Susie, and the chilluns was all wrapped up in me, so I say I'll go. And that how come I'm here, and I ain't never been back, and I ain't see my own sisters and brother and papa since.

We come to New Orleans on the train and take the boat on the Gulf to Galveston and then the train to Hempstead. Mr. Will farm at first and then he and Miss Susie run the hotel, and I stay with them till I gets married to Will Elder in '75, and I live with him till the good Lord takes him home.

I has five chilluns but all dead now, excepting two. I done served the Lord now for sixty-four years, and soon he's going to call old Lucinda, but I'm ready and I know I'll be better off when I die and go to heaven, because I'm old and no-count now.

Henry Banner

Age 89 when interviewed
in 1938 at the county hospital
in Little Rock, Arkansas.

I was born and raised in Russell County, old Virginny. I was sold out of Russell County during the war. Old Man Menefee refugeed me into Tennessee near Knoxville. They sold me down there to a man named Jim Maddison. He carried me down in Virginny near Lynchburg and sold me to Jim Alec Wright. He was the man I was with in the time of the surrender. Then I was in a town called Liberty. The last time I was sold, I sold for $2,300—more than I'm worth now.

I was sold the third year of the war for fifteen years old. That would be in 1864. That would make my birthday come in 1849. I must have been twelve year old when the war started and sixteen when Lee surrendered. Old Man came out on April 9, 1865, and said, "General Lee's whipped now, and damn badly whipped. The war is over. The Yankees done got the country. It is all over. Just go home and hide everything you got. General Lee's army is coming this way and stealing everything they can get their hands on." But General Lee's army went the other way.

I was set free in April. About nine o'clock in the morning, when we went to see what work we would do, Old Man Wright called us all up and told us to come together. Then he told us we were free.

The slaves weren't expecting nothing. It got out somehow that they were going to give us forty acres and a mule. We all went up in town. I went to town and rambled all around, but there wasn't nothing for me.

They asked me who I belonged to and I told them my master was named Banner. One man said, "Young man, I would go by my mama's name if I were you." I told him my mother's name was Banner, too. Then he opened a book and told me all the laws. He told me never to go by any name except Banner. That was all the mule they ever give me. I couldn't get nothing to do, so I just stayed on and made a crop.

Before the war you belonged to somebody. After the war you weren't nothing but a nigger. There wasn't no money. All our money was dead. Nobody had anything. I worked for two bits a day.

Freedom is better than slavery, though. I done seed both sides. The laws of the country were made for the white man. Police were for white folks. Pattyrollers were for niggers. If they caught niggers out without a pass they would whip them. They caught me once in Liberty, and

Mrs. Charlie Crenchaw, old John Crenchaw's daughter, came out and made them turn me loose. She said, "They are our darkies; turn them loose."

One of them got after me one night. I ran through a gate and he couldn't get through. Every time I looked around I would see through the trees some bush or other and think it was him gaining on me. God knows! I ran myself to death and got home and fell down on the floor.

I seen darkies chained. They raised niggers to sell; they didn't want to lose them. If a woman didn't breed well she was put in a gang and sold. Yellow niggers didn't sell so well. Black niggers stood the climate better. At least everybody thought so.

They married just like they do now, but they didn't have no license. Some people say that they done this and that thing, but it's no such a thing. They married just like they do now, only they didn't have no license.

Ida Rigley

Age 82 when interviewed
by Irene Robertson at
Forrest City, Arkansas.

I was born in Richmond, Virginia. Colonel Radford and Emma Radford owned my mother. They had a older girl, Emma, and Betty and three boys. I was younger than her children.

Miss Betty Radford was raising me for a house girl. I called her Miss Betty.

Emma and Betty went to school at Richmond in a buggy. They had a colored-boy driver. He was the carriage driver. Emma and Betty would play with me, too. Miss Betty fed me all the time. She made me a bonnet, and I can't get shed of my bonnet yet. I got four bonnets now.

My mother was Sylvia Jones and she had five children. Mother was a weaver for all on the place. Old Aunt Caroline was the regular cook, but my mother helped to cook for hands he hired at busy seasons of the year.

My sisters lived in the quarters and Mama slept with them. They worked in the field some. They cooked down at the quarters. When Miss Betty went off visiting she would send me down there. I did love it.

They [the Radfords] had a farm right. They had a gin on the place. They had a shop to sharpen and keep all the tools in. We had one spring on the place, I know. One thing we had was a deep-walled well and an ice house. They cut ice in blocks and put it up for winter.

A particular old man made the brooms and rakes. They had a real old man and woman to set about and see after the children and feed them. The older children looked after the babies. The hands got their supplies on Saturday.

Colonel Radford was his own overseer and Charlie his oldest boy. They whipped mighty little. Some of the young ones was hard-headed and rude. He advised them and they minded him pretty well. They would stand up and be whipped. He raised corn, rye, cotton, and tobacco.

They kept hounds. Colonel Radford's boys and the colored boys all went hunting. I'd hear their horn and the dogs. They would come in hungry every time. We had possum and potatoes all along in winter. Eat all you want; possum grease won't make you sick.

We had peacocks, white guinea and big black turkeys, cows, sheep, goats, hogs; he had deer. He kept their horns cut off, and some of the cows' horns wore off.

We had a acre in a garden and had roses and all kinds of flowers. I like flowers now. Tries to have them.

We had goobers and a chestnut grove. We had a huckleberry patch. We had maple sugar to eat. It was good. We had popcorn and chinquapins in the fall of the year. I used to pick up chips to use at the pot. I had a little basket. I picked up corncobs. They burnt them and made corncob soda to use in the bread and cakes. We parched peeled sweet potatoes, slice thin, and made coffee.

During slavery we bought mighty little. Flour in barrels, salt. We had maple sugar and sorghum molasses in bounty. I never seen no whisky. We had cider and wine all along. He had his cider and vinegar press and made wine.

On rainy days all the women would knit, white and colored both. Miss Betty knitted some at night in winter.

Friday was wash day. Saturday was iron day. Miss Betty would go about in the quarters to see if the houses was scrubbed, every week after washing. They had to wear clean clothes and have clean beds about her place. She'd shame them to death.

It seem like there wasn't so many flies. We didn't have no screens. We had peafowl fly brushes. They was mighty pretty. Miss Betty mixed up molasses and flour and poison and killed flies sometimes. She spread it on brown paper. We had fly weed tea to set about, too, sometimes. We didn't have to use anything regular. We had mighty few mosquitoes.

Bill Jones was my father. He was a born freeman and a blacksmith at Lynchburg, Virginia, in slavery time. He asked Colonel Radford could he come to see my mama and marry her. They had a wedding in Colonel Radford's dining room, and a preacher on the place married them.

When the white folks had a wedding it lasted a week. They had a second-day dress and a third-day dress and had suppers and dinner receptions about among the kinfolks. They had big chests full of quilts and coverlets and counterpanes they been packing back. Some of them would have big dances. A wedding would last a week, night and day.

Colonel Radford had a colored church for us all. It was a log house, and he had a office for his boys to read and write and smoke cob pipes in. The white folks' church was at the corner of his place. I went there most. They shouted and pat their hands. Colonel Radford was a Baptist.

Ever so often he had a big dance in their parlor. Dancing was a piece of his religion. He had his own music by the hands on his place. Nearly every farm had a fiddler. He let them have dances at the quarters every now and then. I'd try to dance by myself.

I don't think our everyday frocks was stiffened, but our dress-up clothes was. It was made out of flour—boiled flour starch. We had striped dresses and stockings, too. We had checked dresses.

I seen my best times then. I wish I had that good now. I never got a whipping in my life. I was taught politeness. Miss Betty was good and kind to me. Good as I wanted.

The Civil War was terrible. One morning before we was all out of bed the Yankees come. It was about daylight.

They didn't burn any houses, and they didn't hesitate, but they took everything. They took all Miss Betty's nice silverware. They took fine quilts and feather beds. They took all her nice clothes. She was crying. They was pulling her rings off her fingers.

I told them to quit that. One of the mean things said, "Little nigger, I shoot your head off." They went in another room. I shot under Miss Betty's big skirt. They looked about for me, but they thought I run off to my mama.

That was in the fall of the year. They drove off a line of our slaves a block long, far as from me to that railroad. Made them go. They walked fast in front of the cavalrymen. They took Mama and my sisters. She got away from them with her girls and found her way back to Papa at Lynchburg.

The slaves put their beds and clothes up on the wagons and went off behind them, and some clumb up in the wagons. I heard Miss Betty say, "They need not follow them off, they are already free." The way she said it, like she was heartbroken, made me nearly cry, and I remember her very words till this day. She was a good woman.

Mama come and got me long time after that, and I didn't want to go nor stay neither. It was like taking me off from my own home.

My father was a Presbyterian preacher. I heard Papa preach at Lynchburg. I never knew him very much till long after freedom, and freedom I couldn't understand till I was long grown.

Albert Jones

Age 96 when interviewed
by Thelma Dunston in Portsmouth
on January 8, 1936.

I's pretty old—ninety-six. I was born a slave in Southampton County, but my master was mighty good to me. He wasn't rough—that is, if you done right. But you better never let Master catch you with a book or paper, and you couldn't praise God so he could hear you. If you done them things he sure would beat you.

'Course he was good to me, because I never done none of them. My work wasn't hard neither. I had to wait on my master, open the gates for him, drive the wagon, and tend the horses. I was sort of a house boy.

For twenty years I stayed with Master, and I didn't try to run away. When I was twenty-one me and one of my brothers run away to fight with the Yankees. Us left Southampton County and went to Petersburg. There, we got some food.

Then us went to Fort Hatton, where we met some more slaves who had done run away. When we got in Fort Hatton us had to cross a bridge to get to the Yankees. The Rebels had torn the bridge down. We all got together and builded back the bridge, and we went on to the Yankees. They give us food and clothes.

You know, I was one of the first colored cavalry soldiers, and I fought in Company K. I fought for three years and a half. Sometimes I slept outdoors, and sometimes I slept in a tent. The Yankees always give us plenty of blankets.

The uniform that I wore was blue with brass buttons, a blue cape lined with red flannel, black leather boots, and a blue cap. I rode on a bay-color horse—fact, everybody in Company K had bay-color horses. I took my knapsack and blankets on the horseback. In my knapsack I had water, hardtack, and other food.

During the war some of us had to always stay up nights and watch for the Rebels. Plenty of nights I has watched, but the Rebels never attacked us when I was on.

Not only was there men slaves that run to the Yankees, but some of the woman slaves followed their husbands. They used to help by washing and cooking.

One day when I was fighting, the Rebels shot at me, and they sent a bullet through my hand. I was lucky not to be killed. See how my hand is? But that didn't stop me. I had it bandaged and kept on fighting.

When the war ended I goes back to my master, and he treated me like his brother. Guess he was scared of me, 'cause I had so much ammunition on me. My brother, who went with me to the Yankees, caught rheumatism during the war. He died after the war ended.

Delia Garlic

Age 100 when interviewed
in her home at 43 Stone Street,
Montgomery, Alabama, June 9, 1937,
by Margaret Fowler.

Of her subject, the interviewer writes,
"Unlike many of the old Negroes
of the South, she has no good words
for slavery or the old masters, declaring:
'Them days was hell.'"

I was growed up when the war come, and I was a mother before it closed. Babies was snatched from their mothers' breast and sold to speculators. Chilluns was separated from sisters and brothers and never saw each other again.

'Course they cry! You think they not cry when they was sold like cattle? I could tell you about it all day, but even then you couldn't guess the awfulness of it.

It's bad to belong to folks that own you soul and body; that can tie you up to a tree, with your face to the tree and your arms fastened tight around it; who take a long, curling whip and cut the blood every lick.

I never seed none of my brothers and sisters except Brother William. Him and my mother and me was brought in a speculator's drove to Richmond and put in a warehouse with a drove of other niggers. Then we was all put on a block and sold to the highest bidder. I never seed Brother William again. Mammy and me was sold to a man by the name of Carter, who was the sheriff of the county.

No'm, they weren't no good times at his house. He was a widower and his daughter kept house for him. I nursed for her, and one day I was playing with the baby. It hurt its little hand and commenced to cry, and she whirl on me, pick up a hot iron, and run it all down my arm and hand. It took off the flesh when she done it.

After a while Massa married again, but things warn't no better. I seed his wife blacking her eyebrows with smut one day, so I thought I'd black mine just for fun. I rubbed some smut on my eyebrows and forgot to rub it off, and she cotched me. She was powerful mad and yelled, "You black devil, I'll show you how to mock your betters!"

Then she pick up a stick of stove wood and flails it against my head. I didn't know nothing more till I come to, lying on the floor. I heard the mistess say to one of the girls, "I thought her thick skull and cap of wool could take it better than that."

I kept on staying there, and one night the massa come in drunk and set at the table with his head lolling around. I was waiting on the table, and he look up and see me. I was scared, and that made him awful mad. He called an overseer and told him, "Take her out and beat some sense in her."

I begin to cry and run and run in the night, but finally I run back by the quarters and heard Mammy calling me. I went in, and right away they come for me. A horse was standing in front of the house, and I was took that very night to Richmond and sold to a speculator again. I never seed my mammy any more.

I has thought many times through all these years how Mammy looked that night. She pressed my hand in both of hers and said, "Be good, and trust in the Lord."

Trusting was the only hope of the poor black critters in them days. Us just prayed for strength to endure it to the end. We didn't expect nothing but to stay in bondage till we died.

I was sold by the speculator to a man in McDonough, Georgia. I don't recollect his name, but he was opening a big hotel at McDonough and bought me to wait on tables. But when the time come around to pay for me his hotel done fail. Then the Atlanta man that bought the hotel bought me, too. Before long, though, I was sold to a man by the name of Garlic, down in Louisiana, and I stayed with him till I was freed. I was a regular field hand, plowing and hoeing and chopping cotton.

Us didn't know nothing 'cept to work. Us was up by three or four in the morning, and everybody got they something-to-eat in the kitchen. They didn't give us no way to cook, nor nothing to cook in our cabins. Soon as us dressed, us went by the kitchen and got our piece of cornbread. They wasn't even no salt in them last years. That piece of cornbread was all us had for breakfast, and for supper we had the same. For dinner us had boiled vittles—greens, peas, and sometimes beans. Coffee? No'm, us never knowed nothing about coffee.

One morning I remember I had started to the field, and on the way I lost my piece of bread. I didn't know what to do. I started back to try to find it, and it was too dark to see. But I walk back right slow, and had a dog that walked with me. He went on ahead, and after a while I come on him lying there guarding that piece of bread. He never touched it, so I gived him some of it.

We didn't have no parties, nothing like that. Us didn't have no clothes for going around. I never had nothing but a shimmy and a slip for a dress, and it was made out of the cheapest cloth that could be bought—unbleached cloth, coarse, but made to last.

Just before the war I married a man named Chatfield from another plantation, but he was took off to war and I never seed him again. After a while I married a boy on the plantation named Miles Garlic.

Yes'm, Marster Garlic had two boys in the war. When they went off the marster and mistess cried, but it made us glad to see them cry. They made us cry so much.

Us heard talk about the war, but us didn't pay no attention. Us never dreamed that freedom would ever come.

When we knowed we was free everybody wanted to

get out. The rule was that if you stayed in your cabin you could keep it, but if you left you lost it. Miles was working at Wetumpka [Alabama], and he slipped in and out so us could keep on living in the cabin.

My second baby soon come, and right then I made up my mind to go to Wetumpka, where Miles was working for the railroad. I went on down there and us settled down.

After Miles died I lived there long as I could, and then come to Montgomery to live with my son. I'm eating white bread now and having the best time of my life. But when the Lord say, "Delia, well done; come up higher," I'll be glad to go.